Oracle Application Express by Design

Managing Cost, Schedule, and Quality

Patrick Cimolini

Apress®

Oracle Application Express by Design

Patrick Cimolini
Montreal, Québec
Canada

ISBN-13 (pbk): 978-1-4842-2426-7   ISBN-13 (electronic): 978-1-4842-2427-4
https://doi.org/10.1007/978-1-4842-2427-4

Library of Congress Control Number: 2017958853

Managing Director: Welmoed Spahr
Editorial Director: Todd Green
Acquisitions Editor: Jonathan Gennick
Development Editor: Laura Berendson
Technical Reviewer: Alex Fatkulin
Coordinating Editor: Jill Balzano
Copy Editor: Kezia Endsley
Compositor: SPi Global
Indexer: SPi Global
Artist: SPi Global

Distributed to the book trade worldwide by Springer Science+Business Media New York, 233 Spring Street, 6th Floor, New York, NY 10013. Phone 1-800-SPRINGER, fax (201) 348-4505, e-mail orders-ny@springer-sbm.com, or visit www.springeronline.com. Apress Media, LLC is a California LLC and the sole member (owner) is Springer Science + Business Media Finance Inc (SSBM Finance Inc). SSBM Finance Inc is a **Delaware** corporation.

For information on translations, please e-mail rights@apress.com, or visit http://www.apress.com/rights-permissions.

Apress titles may be purchased in bulk for academic, corporate, or promotional use. eBook versions and licenses are also available for most titles. For more information, reference our Print and eBook Bulk Sales web page at http://www.apress.com/bulk-sales.

Any source code or other supplementary material referenced by the author in this book is available to readers on GitHub via the book's product page, located at www.apress.com/9781484224267. For more detailed information, please visit http://www.apress.com/source-code.

Printed on acid-free paper

Contents at a Glance

About IOUG Press

*IOUG Press is a joint effort by the **Independent Oracle Users Group (the IOUG)** and **Apress** to deliver some of the highest-quality content possible on Oracle Database and related topics. The IOUG is the world's leading, independent organization for professional users of Oracle products. Apress is a leading, independent technical publisher known for developing high-quality, no-fluff content for serious technology professionals. The IOUG and Apress have joined forces in IOUG Press to provide the best content and publishing opportunities to working professionals who use Oracle products.*

Our shared goals include:

- Developing content with excellence
- Helping working professionals to succeed
- Providing authoring and reviewing opportunities
- Networking and raising the profiles of authors and readers

To learn more about Apress, visit our website at **www.apress.com**. Follow the link for IOUG Press to see the great content that is now available on a wide range of topics that matter to those in Oracle's technology sphere.

Visit **www.ioug.org** to learn more about the Independent Oracle Users Group and its mission. Consider joining if you haven't already. Review the many benefits at www.ioug.org/join. Become a member. Get involved with peers. Boost your career.

www.ioug.org/join

Apress®

Contents

About the Author

Patrick Cimolini is a senior computer professional who reaches project goals by understanding and leveraging the relationship between people, procedures, and technology. His Oracle experience began in the early 1990s. His computing career has evolved from the mainframe and client/server eras into today's web-based environment.

About the Technical Reviewer

Alex Fatkulin is a master of the full range of Oracle technologies. His mastery has been essential in addressing some of the greatest challenges his customers have had.

Alex draws on years of experience working with some of the world's largest companies, where he has been involved with almost everything related to Oracle databases, from data modeling to architecting high-availability solutions to resolving performance issues of extremely large production sites.

Alex has a bachelor's of computer science degree from Far Eastern National University in Vladivostok, Russia. He is also an Oracle ACE and a proud OakTable member.

Acknowledgments

First, April Bending, my wife, has supported and encouraged me throughout this project. Without her and her sharp eye for proofreading, this book would not exist.

Second, Insum Solutions Inc. and its supportive team have given me invaluable insights into how people, processes, and technology all work together to achieve results.

Third, the APEX community, whom I have met over the years at various conferences, have fostered an incredible and generous environment of caring and sharing. A special shout-out goes to the APEX development team; without their Herculean efforts and culture of generosity, APEX and its community would not exist.

Introduction

To start, I want to be clear about what this book, *Oracle Application Express by Design,* is about and what it is not about.

The book's main purpose is to list and discuss many of the conflicting design options that are available to an Oracle Application Express (APEX) development team and then encourage the team work out a set of proactive design decisions that are optimal for their project's environment. The book focuses the reader on *how* to best utilize APEX within the context of a large team. Many existing APEX books and blogs focus on granular coding techniques that show developers how to solve specific problems; this book fills a missing niche by showing developers how to assemble their well crafted granular bits and pieces into much larger mosaics of inter-connected code.

Oracle Application Express by Design is crafted to be a catalyst that kick-starts the extremely important interpersonal conversations that must occur between development team members *before* they embark on the task of building a large cloud or enterprise computer application using APEX.

The book is a tool that helps APEX development teams to move through the classic team building stages of:

- *Forming.* Shaking hands, introductions.

- *Storming.* Each team member expresses strong opinions about how to best use APEX.

- *Norming.* Optimal compromises are agreed upon and documented.

- *Performing.* The team pulls together and gets on with the job.

Oracle Application Express by Design is not:

- A Graphic User Interface (GUI) design book.

- A database design book.

- A list of best practices. (The readers must decide what is a "best" practice for themselves in light of their specific environments.)

Now, if you are still with me, let us move on.

What Is APEX?

APEX is a set of procedural language extensions to Structure Query Language (PL/SQL) packages that are installed inside an Oracle database. The APEX PL/SQL code has one prime directive; build an interactive web application on top of an Oracle database. The PL/SQL code does this by performing two fundamental tasks:

- Renders a web page.

- Processes a web page.

An APEX web page is rendered when the PL/SQL code assembles the page description from metadata that is stored in database tables. The page description, which is defined declaratively by the APEX web-based development tool, consists of Hypertext Markup Language (HTML), Cascading Style Sheet (CSS) code, JavaScript, and business data. At its heart, the rendering function uses the following fundamental building block of code to push the page description out to the user's browser:

```
begin
        sys.htp.p('<html>') ;
        sys.htp.p('<body>') ;
        sys.htp.p('Hello Universe!') ;
        sys.htp.p('</body>') ;
        sys.htp.p('</html>') ;
end ;
```

In practice, of course, the code is a lot more complicated. The good news here is that the APEX engine has been carefully optimized for performance so that it adds very little performance overhead to the database.

Processing an APEX web page is done when the user asks the web page to do a full page submit or a partial AJAX page submit by pressing a button or other page activation link. When this happens, the user data is transferred from the web page to the Oracle database where it is validated and safely stored or used to go to the next step in a workflow.

APEX's fundamental architectural simplicity, together with the fact that it is built upon the rock-solid foundations of SQL and PL/SQL, are the reasons that APEX is extraordinarily reliable and stable.

Some of the key characteristics of APEX are:

- No cost feature of the Oracle database

- Declarative tool that is highly productive

- Browser-based development and runtime environments

- Secure

- Scalable

- Fully supported by Oracle

- Friendly, supportive, and accessible user community

APEX Architecture

APEX uses a simple two-tier architecture. The two tiers are:

- *Browser.* The browser works with the code (HTML and CSS) that displays the web page and the code (JavaScript) that controls the user experience.

- *Database.* The database contains the APEX engine (primarily SQL and PL/SQL) that renders and processes the web pages plus the users' business data.

Figure 1 shows how the browser and database tiers fit in the cloud and enterprise environments. The browser and database tiers are linked by a light Java program called Oracle REST Data Services (ORDS). ORDS is a web server that manages the communication protocols between the browser and the APEX engine. ORDS also provides file caching, security, printing tools, and RESTful web services. RESTful web service technology is APEX's window into the wider worlds of the cloud and enterprise.

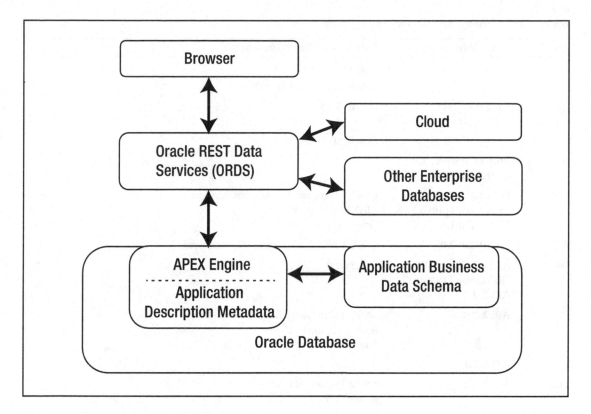

Figure 1. *APEX architecture*

APEX History

History shows us past patterns that can help guide our future. Table 1 lists APEX's major milestones together with some milestones that are important to the technologies that surround and support APEX. The pattern that emerges from this list shows that APEX has developed in step with the external technologies that are intimately entwined with its environment.

APEX was conceived in 1999 as an application called FLOWS at a time when a number of new supporting technologies stabilized. HTML 4.0.1, CSS 2, and the PL/SQL version in Oracle 8i were relatively stable releases. These technologies acted as a springboard for APEX; the original team, Mike Hichwa and Joel Kallman, looked at the technologies and realized that they could build a declarative web development tool; they could "pull it off". A successful proof of concept called Project Marvel was show cased internally to Oracle in 2002.

After several years of development and in-house prototyping, HTML DB 1.5 was released to the public in 2004. This initial release was followed by annual major releases that spanned 2005 to 2012. During this time, HTML DB was rebranded as Oracle Application Express (APEX). By the time it reached APEX 4.2, it has evolved into a reasonably mature and stable web development platform that many organizations saw as a way forward into the worlds of cloud and enterprise computing.

Table 1. *APEX History with Database and Web Contexts*

Year	APEX Milestones	Database & Web Milestones
1998		CSS 2 Oracle 8i (PL/SQL is stable)
1999	Oracle FLOWS (APEX conception)	HTML 4.0.1
2001		Oracle 9i
2002	Project Marvel (APEX birth)	
2004	HTML DB 1.5 (APEX goes public) HTML DB 1.6	CSS 2.1 Candidate Recommendation AJAX Developed Oracle 10g
2005	HTML DB 2.0	CSS 2.1 Reverted back to Working Draft
2006	APEX 2.1 (Rebranded to APEX) APEX 2.2	jQuery 1.0
2007	APEX 3.0	CSS 2.1 Candidate Recommendation jQuery 1.1 and 1.2 Oracle 11g
2008	APEX 3.1	
2009	APEX 3.2	CSS 2.1 updated twice jQuery 1.3
2010	APEX 4.0	jQuery 1.4 jQuery Mobile
2011	APEX 4.1	CSS 2.1 W3C Recommendation jQuery 1.5 to 1.7
2012	APEX 4.2	CSS 3 over 50 modules, 4 published as formal recommendations jQuery 1.8
2013		jQuery 1.9 to 2.0 Oracle 12c
2014		jQuery 2.1 jQuery Mobile 1.4.5 (stable release)
2015	APEX 5.0	
2016	APEX 5.1	Early adopter 1 released in June

The APEX evolution during this time was done against a backdrop of activity in two completely different development worlds that had a profound impact on APEX development.

- *Database.* The database world for APEX is controlled by Oracle. This world has been characterized by steady progress in terms of practical, reliable, and useful new features. The APEX team has developed the database side of APEX in the context of the rock solid Oracle database environment. The SQL and PL/SQL environments are mature, stable, and fast; this foundation is a major reason for the APEX's stability on the server-side backend.

- *Web.* The web world for APEX is controlled by the World Wide Web Consortium (W3C) and the commercial browser manufacturers. This world, due to the open source nature of the W3C, was in a chaotic state during the time that APEX was undergoing its ongoing evolution. For example, in 2004 the W3C released the Candidate Recommendation for CSS 2.1; then in 2004 W3C demoted the recommendation back to working draft. CSS 2.1 was re-promoted back to Candidate Recommendation in 2007. The uncertainty that surrounded the web standards made it exceedingly difficult for commercial developers like the APEX team and browser manufacturers to develop products for the web.

After the release of APEX 4.2 in 2012, the APEX development team embarked on an ambitious development effort to improve the APEX development tool itself. The result was APEX 5.0, which was released in 2015 after a long and difficult development project. Much of the new code was on the web side of the equation; coding for the web and all of the competing browsers was a daunting task, especially in the light of keeping the tool's productive declarative environment intact; thus the multiyear wait for APEX 5.0.

APEX 5.1 followed in 2016. This release added in some of the features that were promised for APEX 5.0 but were dropped due to their impact on the schedule. Going forward, I expect that the new version release cycle will return to an annual event keeping APEX in step with new web and database features that will undoubtedly be released in parallel with APEX.

For a lighter overview of APEX's history, I would like to mention Scott Spendolini's light hearted presentation, "APEX Adolescence," that is available on SlideShare.net at http://www.slideshare.net/sspendol/apex-adolescence?qid=0f5b7637-5c0c-4a7a-946f-0c08855382cf&v=&b=&from_search=13. The slides, which were presented at the Oracle Development Tools User Group (ODTUG) Kscope11 conference, compare APEX's growth to a person's childhood development. The slides follow APEX from conception to adolescence. I interviewed Scott at ODTUG Kscope14 (https://www.youtube.com/watch?v=tKD6mfI4Vfg) and asked where APEX was at the time in terms of childhood development. The answer? APEX 4.2 had grown into a young adult who had just graduated from college. I suspect that Scott would now consider APEX 5.1 to be a mature and experienced working professional.

Where Is APEX Now?

APEX 5.1 is a mature, reliable, stable, and seriously practical web development framework. APEX is a tool that must be on the short list of tools to be evaluated for large, web-based applications that work with an Oracle database and are integrated with the cloud and other enterprise applications.

APEX's strength has been confirmed by Oracle itself. Oracle chose APEX for its shop.oracle.com site, where it sells its products online. This application is the frontend for a suite of very large Oracle E-Business suite applications. As you can see in Figure 2, it has been professionally branded. This proves that APEX succeeds in both the front- and backend coding areas.

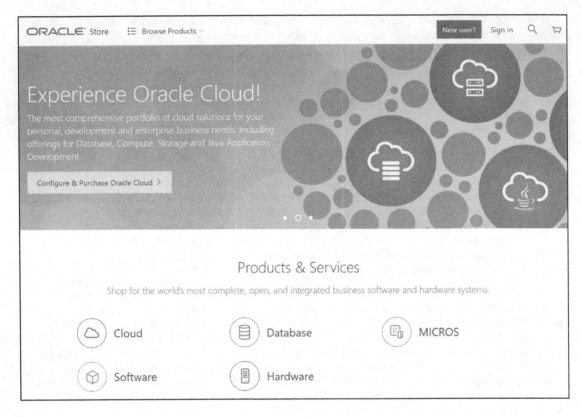

Figure 2. *Oracle's shop.oracle.com site*

Going forward, I see a bright future for APEX, the teams that develop APEX applications, and the organizations that adopt this productive tool.

CHAPTER 1

■ ■ ■

Design Trade-Offs

The act of designing a large and complex artifact like a cloud or enterprise software system is a team sport. A multi-disciplined team of diverse stakeholders must examine the desired artifact from many seemingly conflicting angles and design it in a way that yields the maximum benefit to the company. This is much easier said than done.

Let's put this in perspective by looking at an example that is unrelated to software development; let's look at one aspect of designing an open wheel race car. An open wheel race car is basically an upside down airplane wing. As the car speeds up, the front and rear wings generate a great deal of down-force that pushes the car down into the pavement. This feature is used so that the car can swoosh through corners at high speeds where the high down-force helps it stick to the pavement so that it does not slide sideways. This is good.

On the other hand, down-force on the long, straight parts of a track is bad because the down-force hinders the incredible straight line speeds of which the car is capable. This is bad. So what is the solution? The answer is a trade-off. Yes the car needs down-force, but not too much and not too little. Teams that get the trade-off wrong either spin out in the corners or lose races because they are slow on the straights. Teams that find the "sweet spot" where the car is just fast enough in the corners and just fast enough on the straights go on to win championships.

■ **Note** The word "design" can be used either as a noun or as a verb. As a noun, it is used to describe the artifacts that are the product of a design process. These are things like blue prints, drawings, sketches, process flow diagrams, etc. As a verb, it is used to describe process of creating a design. This book primarily speaks about the verb and uses APEX to illustrate the noun.

© Patrick Cimolini 2017
P. Cimolini, *Oracle Application Express by Design*, https://doi.org/10.1007/978-1-4842-2427-4_1

Stakeholders

Why do cloud and enterprise software systems need trade-offs? Because they must satisfy a large group of stakeholders who all have different and often conflicting wants and needs. Figure 1-1 shows you the rather large list of groups who are affected by a large software system. The figure is a bit of a jumble, which, I believe, represents reality versus the antiseptic classic organization chart. An optimal design must make the appropriate and complex trade-offs in order to maximize the benefits to the overall organization at the expense of individual stakeholder groups.

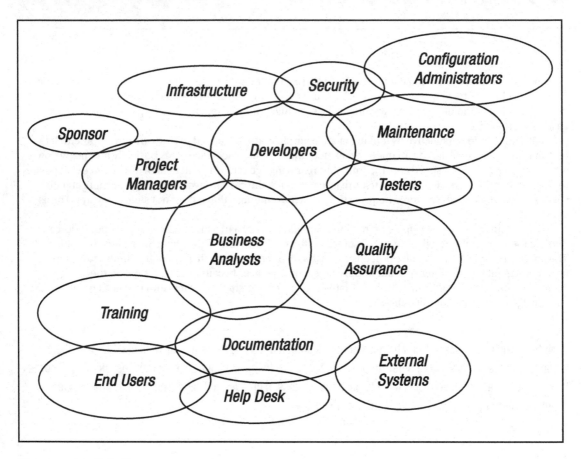

Figure 1-1. *Stakeholders*

Put this in race car terms; you will not need to be the fastest car in the corners and you will not need to be the fastest car on the straights; but at the end of the race, you will need to be the first car across the finish line.

One way to put stakeholder needs in perspective is to ask each stakeholder to define the characteristics of a high quality software system. Table 1-1 lists some of the possible answers to the question, "What makes a software system good?" The table illustrates some of the potential conflicts. For example, the development team might consider a one-page web design to be elegant as it addresses development issues such as no repeated code, easy source code control, all GUI logic in one place, etc. On the other hand, the test and quality assurance teams might hate this design because one minor change to a single page that serves many user roles requires a tedious and costly full regression test that proves that the software still works for all of the roles after the change. The test and quality assurance teams would prefer a design that splits the application into multiple pages, one for each role. These different points of view require some form of trade-off in order to optimize the overall design.

Table 1-1. *Stakeholders Answer the Question, "What Makes a Software System Good"?*

Stakeholder Teams	What Makes a Software System Good?
Sponsor	My company's profit has gone up.
Project Manager	I can easily build a work breakdown structure to track the schedule and costs and manage the resources.
Security	I can easily run automated security tests.
Infrastructure	I do not get calls or e-mails telling me that the system has crashed a server or a database.
Developers	I have developed an elegant solution to a complex problem and the team implemented it on time and within budget.
Maintenance	I can quickly and safely fulfill requests for small changes and small incremental improvements to the system.
Testers	I can quickly check that a function works according to the specification and produce the documentation that proves it works.
Quality Assurance	I sleep well at night because I know that the team has followed our quality assurance process that ensures that appropriate testing has been completed and documented at all stages of development and promotion.
Business Analysts	I can easily verify that the business requirements have been addressed by the system.
Training	I can train end users and system administrators in a short period of time and do not need to give them remedial follow-up courses.
Configuration Administrators	I can configure the system for the test, staging, and production environments through an easy-to-use administration interface.
Documentation	I concentrate on documenting the business rules through an easy-to-use authoring tool that allows me to add online documentation without developer help. I do not need to document the "navigation plumbing" of the system because it is intuitive.
Help Desk	I get few calls regarding the system. When calls do come in, I can quickly solve issues because I have clear documentation for fixing common problems and work-a-rounds for known issues.
External Systems	I can build interfaces to the system because the communication API is reliable and well documented.
End Users	The information I need for decision making is clear and easy to digest. My workflow is clearly laid out so I always know what to do.

Trade-Offs and Quality

Do trade-offs compromise quality? The short answer is "no" and the long answer is, "let's look at the question in more detail so we can be on the same page".

Let's start by looking at Figure 1-2, which illustrates the conundrum of Good, Fast, and Cheap. These are mutually exclusive targets where a "good" artifact will be slow and expensive to build. When you want a fast and cheap artifact, the "good" aspect will suffer. Figure 1-2 is the common way to illustrate the conundrum and it is, unfortunately, very misleading. The Fast and Cheap points on the triangles are well defined points that can be accurately and precisely defined as a date value and a dollar value, respectively. The misleading issue in the figure is the Good point; it is illustrated by a point that leads the viewer to believe that the definition, like Fast and Cheap, can be precisely and accurately defined. This is not reality.

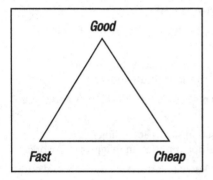

Figure 1-2. *The Good, Fast, Cheap conundrum in theory*

Figure 1-3 is reality. Yes, Fast and Cheap are still represented as accurate and precise points; but Good is illustrated as being open-ended without precision. This reflects the need for trade-offs due to the many different definitions of Good. Note the "line" in the illustration. This represents the concept of "good enough". Many of us, me included, want to strive for perfection; however, striving for perfection compromises schedules and budgets and, from the company's perspective, ignoring schedules and budgets will certainly lead to project failure or worse, bankruptcy. These are bad outcomes for everyone.

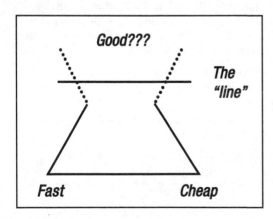

Figure 1-3. *The Good, Fast, Cheap conundrum in practice*

So where do we draw the "line"? It depends on your environment. A good friend of mine learned how to program PL/SQL in the Ukraine where his time was cheap and hardware was expensive. In the Ukraine, he would spend hours and hours shaving nanoseconds off a PL/SQL algorithm. After he moved to the United States, his boss would look over his shoulder and say, "your algorithm is good enough, your time is expensive, and a faster computer is cheap, so please stop chasing nanoseconds." In a different environment there is a different location for the "line".

Now let's go back to the original question, "Do trade-offs compromise quality?" Well, the answer might be "yes" from the perspective of individual bits and pieces; however, the answer must absolutely be "no" from the perspective of the overall package. Individual parts or sub-systems might be compromised slightly due to the trade-offs that must be made to get them to fit into the overall optimal package design; but once the trade-off has been made, the team builds the part or sub-system with the highest quality standards that are allowed within the company's budget and schedule. In car racing terms, no prizes are awarded to cars with the biggest engines or the highest speeds on long straight parts of a race track; prizes are awarded only to race cars that win.

The Human Side of Trade-Offs

I have the honor and privilege to work with a group of very smart, passionate, and hard working teammates who, not surprisingly, have very strong opinions about the "right way" to build things. This is a good situation to be in because it means that I am on a winning team.

Building a winning team that plays hard demands that each player comes to the field with a great deal of emotional maturity. Emotional maturity is mandatory in an environment where players are often asked to play their individual position in a slightly sub-optimal manner in order to support the team's overall optimal strategy. This is often called "taking one for the team"; an act of self sacrifice that is often painful emotionally.

I like to think of our design meetings as a rough contact sport like rugby. After a game, at least half of the bruises, cuts, and scrapes on your body have been inflicted by your own teammates. These hurts were not caused by malicious actions by your teammates; rather, they are innocent side-effects that come with playing a contact sport aggressively. Despite this, a player with a strong sense of emotional maturity will still enjoy a friendly after-game beer with the team and look forward to the next match; the incredible high that comes with winning is worth the price of a bit of pain.

Summary

Large cloud and enterprise software systems must address the needs of stakeholder groups whose needs vary widely and are often in conflict. An ideal design must meet these needs in an optimal manner so that the maximum benefit is realized by the organization rather than individual stakeholder groups. Designing a large system for optimal overall performance requires many trade-offs; often individual pieces must be designed in a slightly sub-optimal manner so that it fits within the larger design. Individual team members, especially software developers, must keep this in mind.

Now that we have had a look at the philosophy of design, let's see how we can apply the theory of optimal overall design to the nitty-gritty practicalities of designing a large cloud-based software system using Oracle Application Express.

CHAPTER 2

■ ■ ■

Inside vs. Outside of the Box

APEX developers constantly refer to working inside or outside of the APEX "box". What does this really mean? Is the choice a significant design consideration? This chapter wrestles with these two questions and gives you a high-level road map that will help guide you when you think you need to venture outside the box.

Working Inside the Box

Working inside the box refers to building APEX applications by using APEX's declarative framework exclusively. Working outside the box refers to using the APEX declarative framework to build a rock solid foundation that underpins custom code and other programming tools that are used to build artifacts that cannot be built directly by the APEX declarative framework. In reality, almost all APEX applications use both approaches; the trick is to know when to take advantage of the efficiency of being inside the box and when you need to step outside of the box and pay the price of higher cost and extended schedules.

Historical Perspective

The box is not static. It has grown by leaps and bounds over the years. One significant illustration of this is the release of Dynamic Actions in APEX 4.0. Before this version, APEX programmers were forced to hand-code a lot of JavaScript and AJAX in order to meet the expectations of their clients. Dynamic Actions put a declarative framework around many of the common Web 2.0 use cases. This dramatically increased the size of the box.

Table 2-1 lists the some of the box-expanding features that have been added to APEX in each major release. This clearly illustrates how the box has grown over time. Looking into the future, I speculate that the expansion trend will continue.

P. Cimolini, *Oracle Application Express by Design*, https://doi.org/10.1007/978-1-4842-2427-4_2

Table 2-1. *How the APEX Box Has Expanded Over Time*

APEX Release	Major New Features
HTMLDB 1.5 - 2004	First public release Declarative web development
HTMLDB 1.6 - 2004	Master Detail wizard Web services Themes/templates
HTMLDB 2.0 - 2005	Session state protection—security Reporting partial page refresh—scalability SQL workshop
APEX 2.1 - 2006	APEX is bundled with the OracleXE free database
APEX 2.2 - 2006	APEX views Component level export Enhanced debugging
APEX 3.0 - 2007	PDF printing Flash charts
APEX 3.1 - 2008	Interactive reports BLOB support Runtime-only installation—security Hidden and protected item type—security JavaScript libraries compressed—performance
APEX 3.2 - 2009	Oracle Forms conversion
APEX 4.0 - 2010	Dynamic Actions Plugins Team development AnyChart 5.1 included RESTful services APEX Listener Integration of jQuery and jQueryUI Tree View page definition APEX Advisor
APEX 4.1 - 2011	Error handling ROWID support Data Upload wizard Enhanced Calendar wizards
APEX 4.2 - 2012	Application Builder for Mobile Mobile and responsive themes HTML5 charts and item types

(continued)

Table 2-1. (*continued*)

APEX Release	Major New Features
APEX 5.0 – 2015	Page Designer Universal Theme and Theme Roller Multiple interactive reports on a page Mobile reporting Modal Dialog pages New Calendar component
APEX 5.1	Interactive grid Master/detail/detail Oracle JET charts

The Box: Pros and Cons

Now let's look at the pros and cons of being inside versus outside of the box. Table 2-2 summarizes some of the key points. When your team starts to discuss the relative merits of things such as simple versus complex architectures, it is important to know that different stakeholders give the individual design issues much different weights. For example, branding the look and feel of a web interface is of little interest to a DBA, whereas it is of extreme importance to the sales and marketing teams who will fight very hard to get a relatively large budget for the branding effort. In other words, when you evaluate the pros and cons of a strategy, do so with the overall enterprise in mind instead of one or two narrow stakeholder perspectives.

Table 2-2. *Pros and Cons of Being Inside or Outside of the Box*

	Pros	Cons
Inside the box	Simple architecture Relatively few moving parts Professional looking interface Acceptable User Experience (UX) Fast development Low development cost Stable applications Easy maintenance Small teams get big results Secure	User interface is not fully branded Limited to APEX's components Many pages Full page refreshes Many extra clicks
Outside the box	Infinite possibilities Explicit branding Granular control over UX	Architecture becomes more complex More moving parts Slower development Higher development cost Risk of instability Difficult to maintain Need larger team with more skillsets Risk of security issues

Designing Inside and Outside of the Box

Now, from a high level, what areas are affected by the inside versus outside the box design choice? The main high level areas are:

- Branding

- User interactions (UX)

- Updating the database

The other, more granular, design areas are covered in detail throughout the rest of the book.

Branding

Branding controls the look of a web site.

Many companies do not have a strong brand that is visible to the world outside of their offices. In this case, APEX provides professional looking interfaces that can that fit well inside the company; minor declarative tweaks can be made to add logos and corporate colors. The Universal Theme has greatly enhanced APEX's declarative branding capabilities.

Companies that have strong, internationally exposed brands will want to take complete control of branding; happily, APEX provides a rich theme and template mechanism that allows graphic designers and GUI professionals to assume complete control over the application look and feel. Figure 2-1 illustrates how an APEX application can be branded by showing you a simple button template. Substitution strings like #LABEL# are owned by APEX. At runtime, the APEX engine replaces the substitution strings with data that it pulls from the application's metadata. Everything else in the template can be owned by the developers, who are free to step outside the box by wrapping the substitution strings in whatever HTML and CSS code that they like.

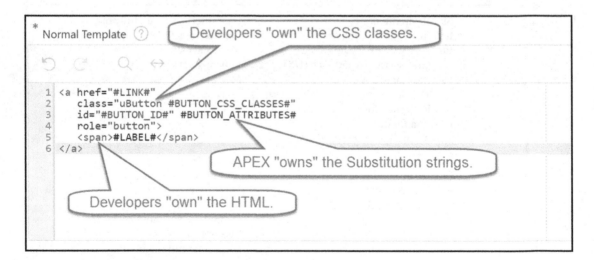

Figure 2-1. *APEX button template*

User Experience (UX)

User Experience (UX) refers to doing something within the browser in response to an action that is initiated by the end user. For example, an end user might make a selection on a page by clicking on an item in a drop-down select list; in response, the interface immediately enables or disables several affected input items. This behavior is easily implemented by an "inside the box" declarative dynamic action that executes JavaScript code in the browser. On the other hand, if the user wants to reorder the line items in a report by simply using a drag-and-drop mechanism, the developer must enhance a dynamic action by writing custom jQuery code because APEX does not provide drag-and-drop as part of its declarative report functionality.

Figure 2-2 shows you the list of Dynamic Action actions that can be taken in response to a user's action on an APEX web page. Many common use cases are handled inside the box by using the Component actions like Clear, Collapse Tree, Disable, and so on. Note that there are two important Execute actions, Execute JavaScript Code and Execute PL/SQL Code. These two actions allow developers to invoke any code that they care to write in the browser or on the server. The Execute PL/SQL action is bundled with a declarative mechanism that exchanges data with the server using AJAX. This is powerful stuff.

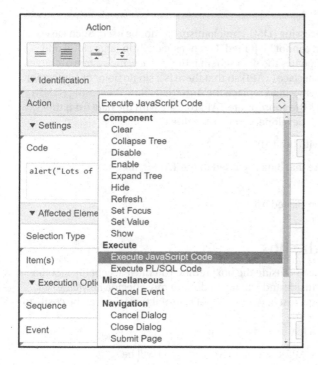

Figure 2-2. Dynamic Action actions

Updating the Database

Updating the database is, of course, the main reason for the existence of APEX. Figure 2-3 shows you the declarative APEX functionality that inserts, updates, and deletes rows in a table. Developers create this process as part of the Create Page wizard that simply asks "what table or view do you want to maintain?" APEX then builds a "Process Row of [table name]" that automatically builds the required Data Manipulation Language (DML) code. This code includes optimistic locking logic that prevents lost updates when two users try to manipulate a table row at the same time. The code that Oracle builds is rock solid and efficient; therefore, APEX developers do not need to spend time testing this aspect of their applications, which is a huge time saver.

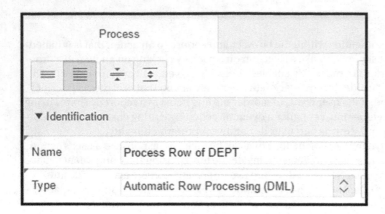

Figure 2-3. *Automatic row processing for a data entry page*

There are cases where the Automatic Row Processing (DML) mechanism cannot be used. Such cases arise when a web page updates multiple tables that cannot be joined. Often, especially in large cloud and enterprise systems, APEX is not the only tool that updates the data schema. In this case, the system architect often specifies a Table Application Programming Interface (TAPI) so that there is a single point of contact for all DML operations. In this case, the APEX developers would replace the Automatic Row Processing (DML) mechanism with a simple PL/SQL process that calls the appropriate TAPI routine with the data from the APEX web page. This mechanism will cost the APEX developers some time due to:

- The learning curve that is associated with the TAPI

- The testing that must be done to ensure that data is passed to the TAPI in the correct format

- Trapping and handling errors that are returned from the TAPI

Road Map for Stepping Outside the Box

The real decision here is not whether to work inside or outside the box; rather, you must accept the fact that you will probably be forced at some point to step outside and when you do, you must decide how far to go and make sure you have a road map so you do not get lost in the myriad of external tools that can be costly to assemble into a solid and reliable system.

How can we approach the decision? Here are a few considerations:

- *Study APEX.* Find out what is inside the APEX box. In many cases you will be pleasantly surprised.

- *Build APEX applications.* Do not try to build Forms, .NET, or Java applications with APEX. Many developers who are new to APEX use development techniques that were well suited to their previous toolset. This usually does not work because a lot of time and cost are wasted by forcing proverbial square pegs into round holes.

- *Show your business analysts how APEX works.* They are generally concerned with results and are happy to frame requirements in a manner that suits APEX when they become familiar with the ways APEX can achieve positive results.

- *Before stepping outside the APEX box, do explicit cost-benefit and risk analyses.* This step is the key to optimizing your design so that it provides maximum benefit to the overall organization.

Summary

The APEX declarative "box" is very large and it is growing with each new version. APEX's declarative framework delivers good looking, easy-to-use, secure, and scalable systems. Teams that build large cloud and enterprise systems that are based on APEX must take the time to educate themselves as to what this efficient and highly productive tool can really do. Extending APEX by moving outside its declarative framework must be done with care; there are legitimate use cases for stepping outside the box, but these trips must be based on realistic technical and business analyses that ensure that the result is optimal for the entire organization.

CHAPTER 3

■ ■ ■

Database Design for APEX

Database design is a huge topic that is well beyond the scope of this book; however, there are some database design issues that must be considered when APEX is used as the primary GUI for managing data in an Oracle database. Some key observations related to database design in an APEX context are:

- APEX lives inside the Oracle database, not in a mid-tier application server.

- APEX itself is a database application that is written primarily in PL/SQL.

- APEX applications are described by metadata that are stored in rows and columns in database tables; they are not described by source code text files that are compiled into executable or WAR files.

Given APEX's tight integration with the database, it is not surprising that there are a few database design issues that are associated with the architecture of a large APEX system. We explore these issues in this chapter.

Primary Keys

Every table in a database must have a primary key. There are a few exceptions, but we do not discuss those here. There are two types of primary key that can be used:

- *Surrogate.* A surrogate key column uniquely identifies a row in a table by using a unique but arbitrary number value. The value is often defined by a database sequence object, a Globally Unique Identifier (GUID), or an identity column (new in Oracle 12c). An index must also be added to the table to ensure that the business data is not duplicated.

- *Natural.* A natural key is a set of real-world data that uniquely defines a row in a database table. A natural key can consist of one column (a social security number for example) or multiple columns (a car part for example), where a number of attributes are combined that uniquely defines the part. Natural keys are also referred to as composite or business keys. The natural key is usually identical in structure to the unique index that is added to a table that employs a surrogate primary key.

The database literature indicates that there is no clear case for using one style of key over the other; there are compelling pros and cons for either choice. When we ask the question, "should we use surrogate or natural keys in our database design?" the answer is always, "it depends". In the APEX world, one of the big "it depends" issues is the fact that APEX plays well with single column surrogate keys; the APEX wizards do a lot of work for you in this case.

© Patrick Cimolini 2017
P. Cimolini, *Oracle Application Express by Design*, https://doi.org/10.1007/978-1-4842-2427-4_3

Most experienced APEX developers will recommend using single column surrogate primary keys when you have the luxury of designing your database schema from scratch. In the real world, however, many new applications are built on top of existing database designs that were constructed using natural primary keys. In these cases, the APEX page and region wizards give you the option of building declarative forms that are based on ROWID, which acts like an invisible single column surrogate key. Figure 3-1 shows you the wizard option that allows you to easily choose your desired type of primary key.

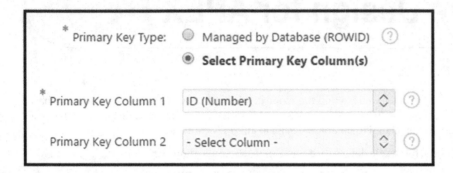

Figure 3-1. *Primary key type selection*

You can build highly functional APEX applications using either style of primary key; however, using single column surrogate keys will save you a bit of extra work when you are building APEX pages and regions using the declarative wizards and when you are building joins in queries. This efficiency can add up to significant time savings when hundreds of tables are involved in your environment.

Column Name Lengths

The length of an Oracle column name can be a maximum of 30 bytes. (However, this limit increases to 128 bytes in Oracle Database version 12.2.) This restriction also applies to APEX item names. These restrictions, on the surface, seem to be in agreement; however, the APEX item naming convention used by the declarative wizards adds a twist to the column naming restriction.

The declarative APEX form wizard automatically creates an item for each column in the underlying table or view. The naming convention for these items is *P<page number>_<column_name>* where *page number* is the page ID and the *column_name* is, well, the name of the column. Figure 3-2 shows you the warning that the APEX advisor gives you when an item name's length is greater than 30. To avoid this situation you should, if possible, pick column names that are 25 or 26 bytes in length so that the *P<page number>_* item prefix can be added by the APEX engine without going over the 30-byte limit. An alternative strategy is to spend time shortening the item names by abbreviating the column name part of the item name. This manual step takes valuable time and breaks the easy-to-remember symmetry between the column and items names.

☑ **Warning** (1)	
☑ Length of Item or Tabular Form Column Name (1)	

Applications > 93686 - Training Hack > Pages > 1 - Home > Regions > Fake Dropdown Button > Page Items > P1_THIS_ITME_NAME_IS_LONGER_THAN_30	
Attribute	Item Name (Identifies a page item and is used to maintain session state. Value may be referenced as a SQL bind variable or using APEX substitution string syntax.)
Check	Length of Item or Tabular Form Column Name
Category	Warning
Message	Name has a length of 35 characters, but should have a maximum of 30 characters.
Value	P1_THIS_ITME_NAME_IS_LONGER_THAN_30
	View

Figure 3-2. *The APEX Advisor warning of a long item name*

Thick Database

APEX is a large set of PL/SQL packages that manipulate data tables that live in a locked schema. This architecture is a classic illustration of the *thick database concept* or paradigm where the underlying details of the database architecture are securely hidden from developers; updates to the schema are done exclusively through a well crafted API. APEX development teams should consider using this architecture when designing their own database schemas that will be maintained by their APEX applications.

There are two principle benefits for using the thick database approach:

- Data integrity

- Performance

Data integrity is ensured by using database components that prevent bad data from entering the data tables. The main data integrity components are:

- Unique indexes

- Constraints

- Foreign keys

- PL/SQL packages that enforce business rules

These components, which are tightly coupled to the database tables, raise errors when users try to enter incorrect data. Are these the only data integrity validations that should be built into a system? No. There are strong arguments for adding client-side validations to a system so that responsive and user-friendly error messages can be crafted to enhance the UX; however, the data integrity rules that are embodied in the database must be considered to be the single source of the truth. A thick database design also acknowledges the fact that your APEX application is not the only source of data updates.

Performance is greatly improved by a thick database design because both the constraint code and the data reside at the same location; they are tightly coupled so that there is no communication overhead between a middle tier logic server and a backend data server. This design eliminates a lot of network traffic and context switching.

There is one area where the thick database design might be relaxed when using an APEX GUI. APEX makes it extraordinarily easy to update base tables and views through its highly productive form creation wizards. Here is a case where careful consideration must be given to the trade-offs between the ideal of a pure thick database design and the construction efficiency that is available to the developers through the declarative APEX features that lend themselves to updating base tables and views directly.

Summary

APEX works well with any well designed database. It works well with both natural and surrogate primary keys; however, working with single column surrogate primary keys makes building APEX applications slightly more efficient. Naming columns with the APEX item name length restriction in mind helps avoid minor name length issues within the APEX environment. How far you go with the thick database design paradigm must be discussed early in a large project; teams must find the optimal set of trade-offs between a pure thick database design and the coding efficiency that accrues from APEX's declarative framework

CHAPTER 4

∎ ∎ ∎

Many Light Pages vs. One Heavy Page

End users want their web pages to load quickly, ideally in under a second. After their web page is loaded, end users then want their web page to be full of artifacts that make their interaction with the page easy and intuitive; and, by the way, they want their pages to have some "pizzazz". As time goes on, end users want their web pages to instantly adapt to changes in their business environment. These goals are in conflict.

Quick load times are achieved by building light and functionally simple web pages. Rich user interfaces are built by adding page components and JavaScript code that cause the page to become large and complex. As pages become larger, the load time becomes longer due to the time it takes to assemble the page on the server, the time it takes to transmit the bytes over the network and through the web server, and the time it takes for the browser to display the page. As pages become more complex, development, maintenance, and testing all become slower and more costly; the risk of error also increases.

So what direction should a team take? In practice, both light and heavy pages are used to varying degrees within a given application or suite of applications; design decisions will be made on a module-by-module basis. This chapter raises some of the issues that must be discussed regarding page design in order to optimize the result.

APEX Wizards Build Many Light Pages

APEX's wizard-driven declarative development framework is one of the major keys to APEX's success. The reasons? Development speed and application stability. The wizards build complete web pages that contain all the plumbing code that is required to:

- Navigate between the wizard built pages
- Extract data from the database
- Display the data in a professional looking and responsive manner
- Pick page items that match the database column data type
- Set the item tab order to match the column ordering in the database

© Patrick Cimolini 2017

P. Cimolini, *Oracle Application Express by Design*, https://doi.org/10.1007/978-1-4842-2427-4_4

- Display pop-up help when the database columns contain comments and the user interface defaults are enabled for the table

- Validate user input when database constraints are present

- Safely tuck the data into the secure arms of the Oracle database

The APEX engine does a tremendous amount of plumbing work for the developer, who can run through many of the wizards in under 60 seconds. Developers can then concentrate their minds on the "real" work, which is adjusting the page layout to avoid scrolling and adding the business rule logic. For many hard-nosed business owners, this is all that is required to "get the job done"; hard-nosed business owners tend to see anything more as stepping into the area of diminishing returns.

Figure 4-1 illustrates the result that is achieved by using APEX's "Form on a Table with Report" wizard. A key feature of this two-page architecture is the fact that each page does only one task and does it extremely well. The report page displays an interactive report; it does nothing else. The form page displays a single database record so that the user can process the record or create a new record; it does nothing else. The strategy of using wizard-based development makes application construction fast; however, it tends to build applications that contain many individual single function pages that ask the database server to build them from scratch every time the pages are accessed. It is important to note that the APEX engine is extremely efficient and fast when it is asked to build a light, single-purpose page. In addition, the end user must click a lot to see individual snippets of the data that they need in order to get their jobs done. This architecture tends to present individual trees to the end user without showing them the forest.

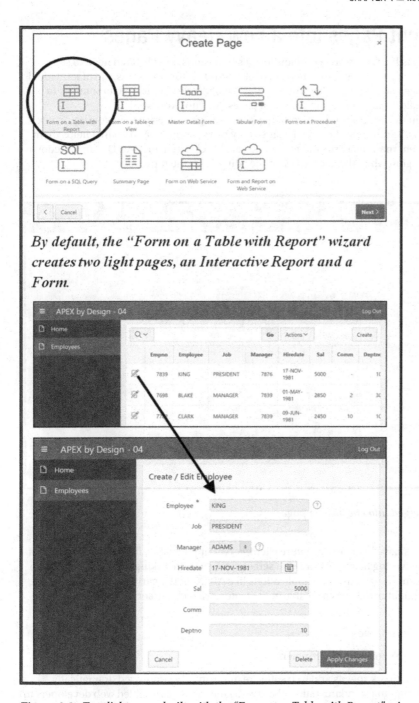

By default, the "Form on a Table with Report" wizard creates two light pages, an Interactive Report and a Form.

Figure 4-1. *Two light pages built with the "Form on a Table with Report" wizard*

Merging Many Light Pages into a Few Heavy Pages

Senior end users who are responsible for making complex business decisions quickly often need to see a large amount of disparate data simultaneously; they need to back up and see the forest instead of individual trees. These users need web pages that both display and process a lot of data from many data sources. In these cases, the strategy that builds many single-purpose light pages does not work well.

Figure 4-2 shows a first step toward combining two single-purpose light pages into one multi-purpose heavier page. End users tend to like this type of design because they can see summary data that helps them enter the detail data in an efficient manner. Performance can be very quick when an AJAX Dynamic Action is used to refresh the data entry region when the user clicks on the edit icon in the report.

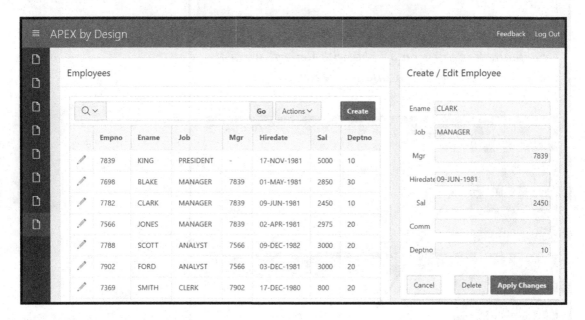

Figure 4-2. *Two light pages merged into one heavier page*

For many years, senior users have been using mature client/server applications, like Oracle Forms, that have done a very good job of delivering heavy, feature-rich screens. Now we are asking these senior users to move from client/server applications to web-based applications like APEX. In the early days of the web, it was difficult to mimic the functionality that was available in the feature-rich client/server applications. The difficulty was due to:

- Relatively slow network speeds

- Immaturity of the web's software environment

Over the last two decades, network speeds and web software maturity have improved dramatically. Fiber optic technology and the ongoing standardization of the web languages has enabled web developers to start delivering web applications that are coming close to providing user experience features that were taken for granted in the older client/server world. Going forward, even greater improvements in web hardware and software technologies will make it easier for developers and their tools to provide end users with a rich user experience on the web.

This trend toward building heavy pages that provide a rich user interface is clearly illustrated by APEX itself. APEX 4.2 and its earlier versions were designed with the "many light pages" strategy. Over time, as the APEX developer community started to build larger and larger applications, they started to grumble about this architecture because in order to make a change that affected a large number of items on a single page, they had to navigate to the edit page for every item on the page and repeat a change for each and every individual item. This was a tedious and error-prone task.

APEX 5.0 introduced the Page Designer (see Figure 4-3) development page; this is a single heavy page that contains a tremendous amount of functionality. One of the principal benefits of this design is the ability to highlight many items on the left side of the page and then change attributes that are common to all of the items by setting the value of the attribute once on the right side of the page.

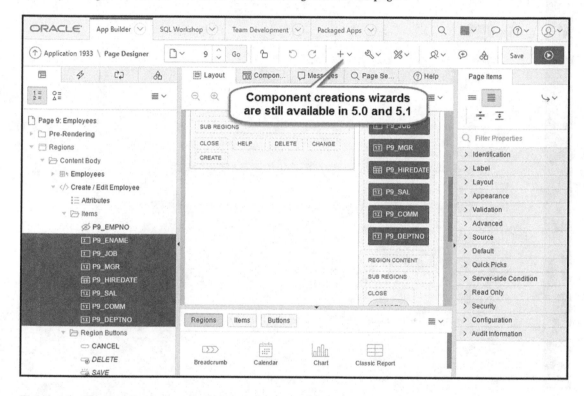

Figure 4-3. *The Page Designer, a single heavy, feature-rich page*

The page designer gives an APEX developer, who is a sophisticated computer user with a high degree of business knowledge, the ability to:

- See a great deal of information about the page that is being constructed or maintained

- Work through multiple complicated workflows

The Page Designer's single heavy page design is a strategy that has significantly increased the productivity of APEX developers.

It is important to note here that casual APEX developers who are not using APEX as a full time job have not been forgotten. The Page Designer contains a menu icon that exposes links to multi-page wizards that step the casual developer through the processes to build components like pages and regions. The individual steps ask the user to input the most important and common attribute values for the component that is being built. These wizards are an important feature for casual APEX developers and developers who are new to the tool. These developers generally appreciate the explicit assistance that the wizards provide.

APEX 5.1 introduced the Interactive Grid (see Figure 4-4). This APEX page component contains a lot of functionality for both developers and end users. When it comes to designing APEX pages and applications, it is a game changer.

Figure 4-4. *Multiple Interactive Grids on one page*

Developers can build an Interactive Grid declaratively in a minute or two. The follow-up work of configuring user interface components for individual columns and setting up data validations is also declarative, which means that development of this powerful component is easy and fast. Maintenance programming is also straightforward and almost risk free. Testing the Interactive Grid itself has already been done by Oracle; therefore, the testing and quality assurance teams can concentrate on looking at the business rules that are associated with the Interactive Grid; they do not need to rigorously test the mechanical plumbing associated with the Interactive Grid's interaction with the database.

Senior end users are happy with the Interactive Grid. It is a robust component that allows them, on a single page, to maintain data using multiple feature-rich grids that interact with multiple data sources. A great deal of data and functionality can be exposed without needing a lot of navigation clicks.

The main take-away here is that the Interactive Grid has the potential to dramatically increase productivity for both the developer and end user communities.

Light Pages vs. Heavy Pages: Picking the Correct Strategy

So how should we build APEX applications? The answer, of course, is trite; "it depends". Now let's look at some of the "it depends" issues.

Designing for End Users

Many developers think that the term "end user" refers to a single group of individuals. This might be true for small departmental APEX applications, but it rarely applies to a large cloud/enterprise application. Large applications tend to have a large user community that is made up of sub-groups that have diverse needs and skillsets. Figure 4-5 is a matrix that illustrates end user needs based on a simplistic view of two skillsets—computer skills and business knowledge.

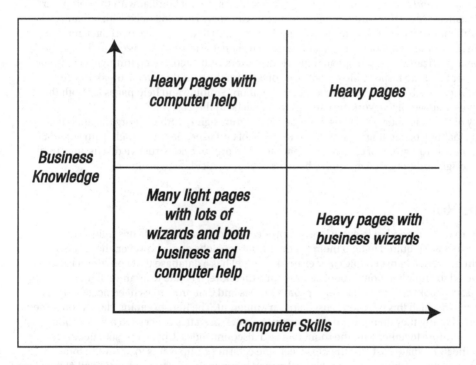

Figure 4-5. *Deigning for end users with different skillsets*

High computer skills and high business knowledge: These users are the application's "super users". They probably use the application for many hours per day. They are intimately familiar with the business and are experienced computer users who can effectively take advantage of many implicit computer productivity enhancements like keyboard shortcuts and right-click context menus. They do not need or want the GUI to hold their hands or spoon feed them. They want to get their work done quickly and accurately with the fewest mouse and keyboard interactions as possible. They are comfortable with taking professional responsibility for their interactions with the application. A heavy page design that shows a lot of data and is capable of performing many workflow steps is highly desirable for this class of user.

Lower computer skills and high business knowledge: These users may be business managers or front-line personnel who must occasionally work with the application. They know the business so they probably understand the terminology that is presented on the application pages and know the workflow results that are expected; however, they are probably not familiar with some of the GUI's productivity widgets that perform unexpected "magic" when tabbing between input fields. These users can probably use the heavy page design providing that online help is provided to them so that they can refresh themselves on how the page's widgets work. Accuracy is the primary objective here; they want to get the job done and get it done correctly. Speed is usually not a big consideration.

High computer skills and lower business knowledge: These users may be senior technical or business personnel who, for example, are asked to help a business unit to which they do not belong. They tend to be skilled at using the computer application because it is similar to the applications that they use in their regular business unit; however, they will not be familiar with the terminology, data, and the workflow in the new business unit. These users would not be intimidated by a heavy page providing that business help was easily accessed. Also, a strong case could be made for building wizards that step through the business workflows; this is, in a way, like adding help pages. Again, accuracy is more important than efficiency for these users.

Lower computer skills and lower business knowledge: These users are not familiar with the computer technology or the business; casual and junior personnel fit this category. They will need a lot of hand holding in order for them to get the work done accurately. Heavy pages that contain a lot of data and the ability to perform many workflow actions are actually dangerous here because of the risk of making a mess that is costly to clean up. Wizards can be of great help to junior users who need to step through a complete workflow. When junior users are responsible for only one or a few of the workflow steps, breaking the application into multi-page sub-modules might be a consideration. Training and help pages for both the computer and business aspects of the work are extremely beneficial in this case.

The probability of the exact four quadrants discussed here fitting tightly with your organization is low; however, the probability of needing to go through this type of end user analysis is high. I am sure that presenting a similar matrix to a group of engaged stakeholders will produce constructive discussions that will lead to a set of design trade-offs that maximize benefits to your particular environment.

Designing for Roles

The concept of user roles is embedded in every large computer application. Each role has unique data and workflow needs that are required to help them get their front-line jobs done; however, there can be a significant amount of overlap between roles. For example, a hotel has a database that contains a list of rooms. Most roles need to know if a room is booked or empty; therefore, it is safe to assume that a boolean function called is_room_booked(p_room_number, p_date) exists and that most roles need access to this function. The contexts in which this function is used are very different. The housekeeping staff is concerned with only the current day and they do not need the room rate. Check-in staff is concerned about a room's availability in the near future together with the room rate and discount codes. Check-out staff needs the room charges from the immediate past. For the next week, the catering group wants to know the total occupancy so that the restaurant food and beverage orders can be right-sized. You can see that all of the hotel staff need access to the room database but that they need different views of the data and they have different workflows.

How do we approach design for this situation. At a high level, we have two very fundamental choices:

- Build many light pages that are each tailored to a specific role

- Build one heavy page that is shared by all the roles; control what is presented through authorization schemes

These design approaches are the extreme ends of a wide spectrum; practical designs often fall somewhere between the two extremes, whereby applications are divided into related modules that, in turn, are shared by related roles.

What is the impact of choosing a light or heavy page design relative to end user roles? It depends on the stakeholder viewpoints.

End users: A well crafted authorization design hides artifacts that belong to other roles; therefore, end users don't know or care if their application pages support one or multiple roles. They just want to get their work done.

Construction developers: APEX projects are unique because they are constructed in unique businesses that have unique targets and constraints. A light page strategy can be the correct choice where the application must be built quickly with a small budget; in this case, the developers will tend to build pages using the APEX wizards exclusively which will, by default, tend to build a lot of light pages. A heavy page strategy can be the correct choice where the application contains components and business rules that are liberally shared across many roles and modules; in this case developers will want to minimize code repetition by bundling common data and logic in a small number of pages that are shared my many roles. Constructing a rich user experience will also be factored into the design choices. The choice between light and heavy page construction is almost never an "all or nothing" choice; most large applications contain a mix of strategies because each module will have a unique set of users with unique skillsets.

Maintenance developers: When asked to add or change a relatively simple component on an existing page, maintenance developers want to be able to do the task quickly and accurately with very little risk of breaking existing functionality. A light, single role page lends itself well to this type of work because of the inherent simplicity. For example, adding a check box should be a simple one hour job. On the other hand, if the page supports two or more roles that require a complex authorization setup together with many Dynamic Actions that are specific to the roles, adding a simple check box might require much more than the estimated hour. Why? The maintenance developer must first understand how the page works so that adding the new check box and its associated logic does not break the existing logic. Taking two days to complete a supposedly one hour task looks terrible on an employee's performance review, so I would argue that maintenance developers vote for a simple, one role, and very light page design.

Testers: High-quality testing is hard technically and emotionally. It is difficult technically because the testers need to construct a large suite of usage scenarios and then automate them. It is difficult emotionally because the same set of tests must be run again and again with small adjustments, even when the application changes are small. The testing effort for light, single-purpose and single role pages is relatively easy; the light pages are responsible for a limited set of actions so testing is done relatively quickly. On the other hand, heavy pages that support many roles, contain rich user experience code, display a lot of data, and contain many workflow actions can be difficult and time consuming to test. An added difficulty comes into play in industries that are heavily regulated, like banks and nuclear power stations. In these industries, not only does the testing need to be done, explicit evidence that proves that the testing was done needs to be provided. I suspect that testers and quality assurance folks prefer a light page strategy so that they can test small changes in a small amount of time.

Performance Issues

Now what about performance? Web applications must transmit every piece of data and logic across the network from the server to the browser. This takes time and design compromises must be made between the requirement for sub-second response times and the requirement for a rich user interface. Figure 4-6 sets the stage for this discussion.

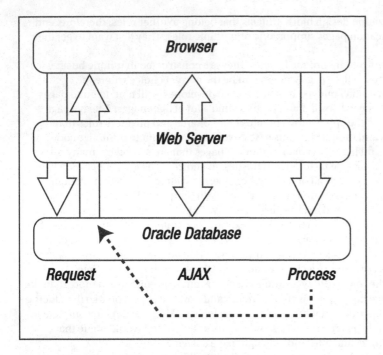

Figure 4-6. *A day in the life of an APEX page*

There are three basic interactions between the browser and the database. The high-level conversations go something like this:

Request: The browser says to the server, "Please send me a page". The server responds by assembling the page and sends the complete page back to the browser over the network through the web server (there is more about the web server later, when we get into the details).

AJAX: The browser says to the server, "Something happened here, please do a bit of work for me with the attached data and send me the result so I can update only the bit on the page that needs it". The server does the requested work and ships the result back to the browser. This strategy is much faster than performing multiple full page refreshes that reload page areas that did not change.

Process: The browser says to the server, "The end user is done with this page. Here is all of the data on the page. Have fun. Oh, and by the way, if the end user has honked things up, please let me know so I can slap them on the wrist." The server rolls up its sleeves, displays the "I am busy" icon and begins validating and processing the data. If all goes well, the validated data is stored safely in the application's base tables and the cycle begins again when the server sends the next page to the browser.

Now let's look at these conversations with a bit more seriousness and detail.

Request

End users request a page when they click on a link or tap on a button. The request, which is formatted as a short URL string, passes from the browser, through the web server, and into the Oracle database, where control is given to the APEX engine.

The transmission over the network and through the web server is fast and is rarely the cause of a performance problem. The web server layer converts the URL into a form that is understood by the APEX engine and also manages the security duties that are related to reverse proxies and firewalls. This step is also fast.

Potential performance concerns in the request action can arise in three areas when the requested page is heavy:

- Building the web page dynamically in APEX engine

- Transmitting the web page from the server, through the web server, and out to the browser

- Setting up the code and displaying the page in the browser

Figure 4-7 is a schematic that shows the work that the APEX engine does when it receives a request to build a page.

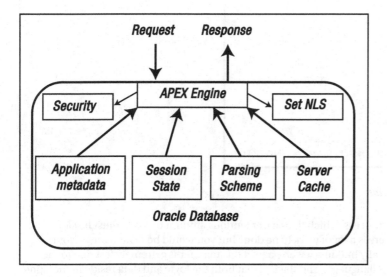

Figure 4-7. *The APEX engine at work*

The first order of business is the repetitive housekeeping that is done for every web page request; the engine must check security to make sure that the request is coming from an authenticated user and it must set up the National Language Support (NLS) parameters for the database session.

After the housekeeping is done, the work of assembling the web page starts. The APEX engine reads the URL request string and then queries the APEX metadata to get the template for the desired page. Figure 4-8 is a screenshot of the first few lines of the header and body definitions of the Universal Theme's standard page template. Templates are a mix of HTML code and substitution strings like #TITLE#. The APEX engine will replace #TITLE# with the title of the application, while the #SIDE_GLOBAL_NAVIGATION_LIST# will be replaced with another template that contains its own HTML code and substitution strings. Template nesting can be very deep. The APEX engine reads the templates and resolves the substitution strings by reading data from the application's metadata, session state, and the parsing schema. The HTML code and data are dynamically assembled into strings that are passed as parameters to the function, sys.htp.p, which pushes the web page out to the web server.

```
Definition

* Header (?)

  ↺   ↻    Q   ↔   A̅

1  <!DOCTYPE html>
2  <html class="no-js #RTL_CLASS# page-&APP_PAGE_ID. app-&APP_ALIAS." lang=
3  <head>
4    <meta http-equiv="x-ua-compatible" content="IE=edge" />
5    <meta charset="utf-8">
6    <title>#TITLE#</title>
7    #APEX_CSS#
8    #THEME_CSS#

* Body (?)

  ↺   ↻    Q   ↔   A̅

1  <div class="t-Body">
2    #SIDE_GLOBAL_NAVIGATION_LIST#
3    <div class="t-Body-main">
4      <div class="t-Body-title" id="t_Body_title">
5        #REGION_POSITION_01#
6      </div>
7      <div class="t-Body-content" id="t_Body_content">
8        #SUCCESS_MESSAGE##NOTIFICATION_MESSAGE##GLOBAL_NOTIFICATION#
```

Figure 4-8. *Definition of a page template*

You might start to think that this process, which does a tremendous amount of work, must be slow. You would be correct in saying the there is a lot of work to be done but you would be dead wrong about the "slow" bit. The process of dynamically building a web page in this manner is extremely fast due to the inherent speed of the SQL and PL/SQL languages and the fact that both the logic and data reside in the same database; there is no need for data transmission between different tiers.

■ **Note**   Michael Hichwa, the "father" of APEX, presented a delightful talk at the APEX Connect 2016 conference in Germany. The talk is titled "APEX Vision, Past, Present, Future". During the talk, Mike spoke about gathering and presenting empirical data to skeptical Oracle executives who did not think that it was possible to dynamically assemble and deliver web pages in a performant manner. The data proved that it could be done. The presentation is available on YouTube.com and, since you are obviously interested in APEX, I highly recommend that you view it.

https://www.youtube.com/watch?v=i_5OUipxSEY

Possible performance issues usually arise when developers pull data from the parsing schema. A SQL query like select * from EMP will execute extremely quickly; EMP is a small table with a single column primary key. Performance problems will arise when the developers must pull data from a large number of data tables that contain many rows. This is not an APEX issue; it is a database design issue. Queries that are developed by the construction developers are probably the chief source of performance issues and should be one of the first things to be checked. A deep dive into database design is out of scope for this book because the topic is well covered in the literature.

APEX provides access to a server cache that stores pre-assembled APEX components like regions. If a region contains information that rarely changes—help and breadcrumb regions for example—then you can ask APEX to store the assembled version so that the engine does not need to rebuild it from scratch every time the page is requested. This helps performance. Figure 4-9 shows the available options for this feature together with the settings that give you granular control over whether a fresh version of the component is used instead of the cached version.

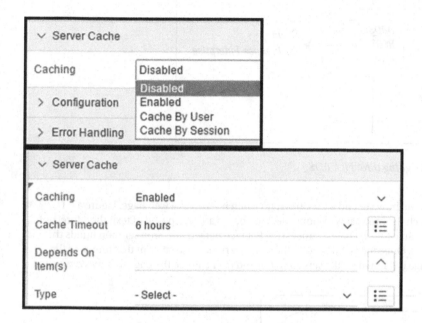

Figure 4-9. *Server Cache options and settings for a region*

Now what happens when a response goes through the web server on its way out to the browser? Figure 4-10 is a high level view of the Oracle REST Data Services (ORDS) mid-tier application. ORDS does several things to an APEX web page before it is sent on its way out to the browser. It:

- *Replaces URL placeholders like* `c:\APEX050000\i\` *with static files that are stored on the web server's hard drive or, better yet, in the server's cache memory.* Note that the static files can also be stored and retrieved from the Oracle database itself. This is sometimes desirable in a development environment where developers do not have easy access to the web server; however, the files should be moved to the web server hard drive in test and production environments to optimize speed.

- *Communicates with external cloud and on-premise enterprise applications through RESTful data services that rely on JavaScript Object Notation (JSON).* Pay attention to this area because many organizations are quickly moving to the cloud and replacing on-premise DB links with RESTful services. Also note that APEX 5.0 introduced the PL/SQL API package called APEX_JSON, which makes working in this area fast and efficient.

- *Converts parts of the data stream into a printable format by invoking the Formatting Objects Processor (FOP).* This functionality is still fairly basic at the writing of this book. Other options for converting data into printable formats are mentioned in Appendix B.

Once the infrastructure team has set up a web server, it usually runs efficiently and adds very little overhead to the overall web page delivery process.

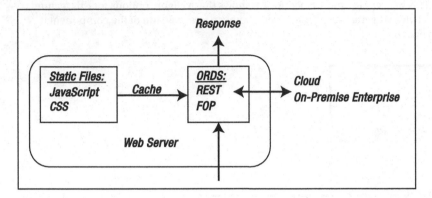

Figure 4-10. *An APEX response going through ORDS*

Now we need to ask about the browser and what does it do when it receives a web page. Figure 4-11 outlines the major tasks for which the browser is responsible. Web pages are composed of text; therefore, not surprisingly, the browser must parse the text before processing it. Once parsed, the browser then builds the Document Object Model (DOM). Once the DOM is built, the browser runs the JavaScript that prepares the page if required. Finally, the page is painted on the screen so the end user can see the page that was requested.

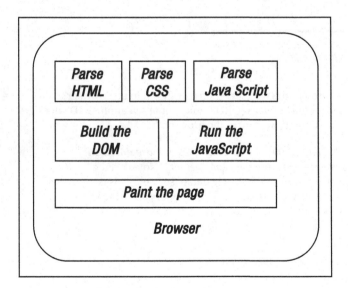

Figure 4-11. *Browser tasks required for rendering an APEX page*

The browser can cache web pages on the end user's computer, tablet, or phone. While this strategy can dramatically improve performance, Oracle recommends that this feature be turned off for security reasons. Generally, APEX applications that pull data from an Oracle database contain some sensitive data that should not be stored locally on a computer, where it can be accessed later by non-authorized end users long after the legitimate user has logged off.

AJAX

Asynchronous JavaScript and XML (AJAX) is a seductive technology. It helps enormously when GUI architects and developers design web pages that give end users a rich and responsive User Experience (UX). In a nutshell, AJAX is a set of JavaScript tools that allows a web page to ask the server for a small piece of data that updates only a small part of the web page. This is referred to as a partial page refresh as opposed to a full page refresh, which requires a full request and response cycle that builds the entire web page.

There are two aspects to consider when building APEX pages that depend heavily on AJAX:

- The initial page load time can be significant when the page is very heavy due to the presence of many GUI artifacts that are designed to give the end user a rich UX.

- Once the page is loaded in the browser, the end user experiences very fast responses in response to their actions. For example, an end user might make a selection from a drop-down list and an AJAX call to the server might bring back some calculated supporting information that is related to the choice.

An optimal design must balance the pain of the initial load time against the efficiency and productivity of the rich UX that is based largely on AJAX calls. An excellent example of this trade-off is found in APEX 5.0. Figure 4-12 shows the page load statistics for the same page that is loaded by the light component view versus the heavy page designer view. In this specific case, the page designer takes almost a second and a half longer to load. For most APEX developers, the wait is more than made up for by incredible productivity boost that the heavier page designer gives them through its aggressive use of JavaScript and AJAX.

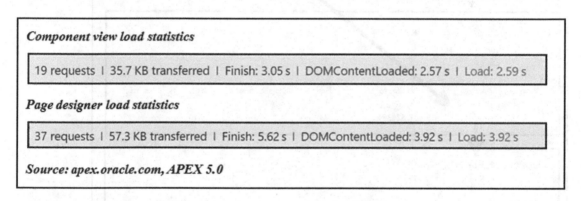

Component view load statistics

19 requests | 35.7 KB transferred | Finish: 3.05 s | DOMContentLoaded: 2.57 s | Load: 2.59 s

Page designer load statistics

37 requests | 57.3 KB transferred | Finish: 5.62 s | DOMContentLoaded: 3.92 s | Load: 3.92 s

Source: apex.oracle.com, APEX 5.0

Figure 4-12. Load statistics for the component view versus the page designer

Process

When end users have completed their interaction with the GUI, they submit the page data for processing. The browser is asked to assemble the data into a format that can be transmitted back though the web server to the database server. The APEX engine must, just as it did with a simple request, verify the end user's credentials and set up the NLS parameters. After that, the engine steps through the following tasks:

- Copies all of the browser data into the appropriate session state variables so that the data is accessible to the downstream processing.

- Validates the data and notifies the end user when errors are found.

- Manipulates the data if required according to business rules before saving them in the application's base tables.

- Saves the data in the application's base tables and/or performs work flow tasks within the database.

- Branches to a page and starts the request and response cycle again.

The action here is inside the database and is generally not affected by the light versus heavy page design decision.

Measuring Performance

Quantitative data always helps when you are making design decisions. Consider building a couple of "proof of concept" applications, one with light pages and one with heavy pages, before embarking on building a large, expensive APEX application so that you can gather the quantitative data that will be a big part of shaping your design decisions.

On the server side, APEX gives you a debug view that shows, step by step, how an APEX page is built. Figure 4-13 shows you what the debug page looks like and highlights the timing column. It shows you explicitly where performance issues are located. The debug page is accessed by toggling the Debug/No Debug link in the developer toolbar and then selecting View Debug.

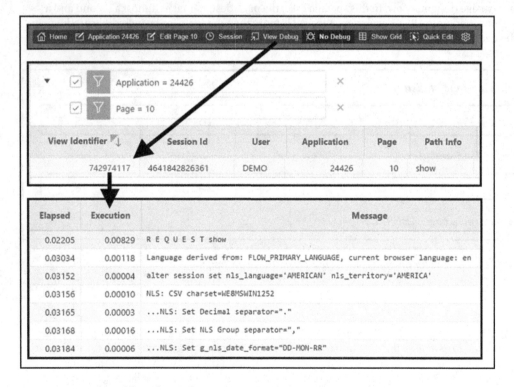

Figure 4-13. *APEX debug shows the server timing for building an APEX page*

All of the mainstream modern browsers contain developer tools that measure response times from the browser's perspective. These tools should be used in conjunction with the APEX server-side tool to get a complete performance picture. Figure 4-14 shows you Chrome's developer tool displaying the network data; Figure 4-15 shows a screenshot of the timeline page. Both pages provide insight to the work that is being done on the network and inside the browser. The details here are beyond the scope of this book; however, reading the Chrome's developer tool documentation is mandatory for understanding the complex data that is being displayed.

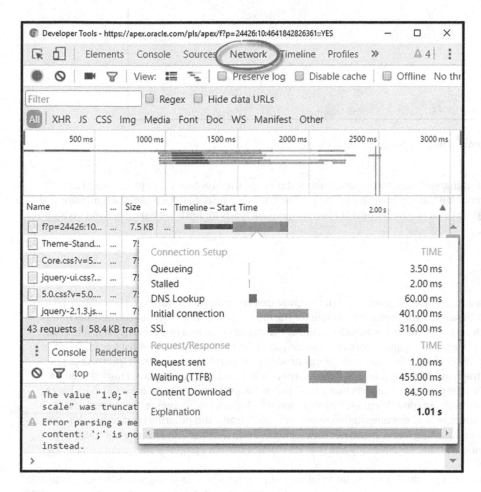

Figure 4-14. *Chrome's Network tab for an APEX page*

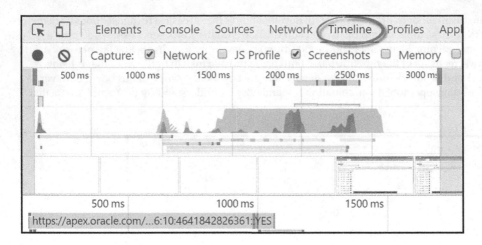

Figure 4-15. *Chrome's Timeline tab for an APEX page*

After you have gathered quantitative performance data from the proofs of concept, you need to present the data to the DBA and infrastructure teams. They will use the data to estimate the hardware and software configurations that will be required to handle the peak loads for both the light page and heavy page scenarios.

Summary

Choosing between a many light page and a few heavy page design strategies is not easy when you need to optimize the result to achieve the maximum benefit for the organization. The end user community needs to be analyzed with respect to their business knowledge, computer skills, and numbers in each sub-group. Some user groups prefer heavy pages where they can do most of their work quickly with a minimum of keystrokes and mouse clicks, while other user groups need lots of help from many single-purpose pages that lead them by the hand through the work flows. Authorization roles play a big part in page design. Is it better to build a single page that supports many roles like accounts receivable and accounts payable or should you build multiple, single role pages? Construction developers, maintenance developers, testers, quality assurance, trainers, and documentation teams will have strong and differing opinions in this area. Performance; how do light and heavy pages perform relative to one another? End users want the speed of light pages combined with the functionality and user experience of heavy pages—"they want to have their cake and eat it too".

Now what is the best practice? Light or heavy? The best practice lies in knowing well your technical and human environment and making tough and hopefully optimal trade-offs.

CHAPTER 5

■ ■ ■

Database Updates

The data inside a database is an extremely valuable asset when it accurately models a business. Accurate data enables an enterprise to study and learn from past performance, make today's business decisions based on reliable real-time evidence, and step into the uncertain future based on realistic forecasts. Inaccurate data, on the other hand, is a disaster because business decisions will be made on the basis of fantasy instead of fact, which often leads to business failure.

It is clear that the prime directive of a computer system is to guarantee that the data it manages is accurate at all times. This chapter explores this issue from an APEX perspective; however, in larger cloud and enterprise environments, APEX is only one of several tools that maintain the data. In light of this, the mechanisms that update the data must account for the usage of multiple technologies.

The main objectives of technologies that maintain data in a database are:

- Data accuracy (the prime directive)

- Performance

- Security

If the data is inaccurate, tuning the database for performance is a waste of time. Security, however, is a mandatory effort because inappropriate disclosure of data, even if the data is inaccurate, can be costly to the enterprise.

The technical teams who need to be involved in this conversation are developers, DBAs, infrastructure, and the security team.

Architecture

First, we must explore the architecture of the access mechanism that is used to maintain the data inside a database. Bryn Llewellyn, Oracle's product manager for PL/SQL, wrote a whitepaper in November 2016 that is titled, "Why Use PL/SQL?" (`https://blogs.oracle.com/plsql-and-ebr/resource/Why_Use_Plsql_Whitepaper_10.pdf`). This whitepaper makes a very strong ("unassailable" in Bryn's words) case for using a thick database paradigm. This chapter is largely based on Bryn's whitepaper and I strongly recommend that you take the time to read it.

© Patrick Cimolini 2017
P. Cimolini, *Oracle Application Express by Design*, https://doi.org/10.1007/978-1-4842-2427-4_5

Figure 5-1 illustrates the three layers inside an Oracle database that make up a thick database environment. The client software is most often located outside the database. APEX is a notable exception; however, even though APEX is physically inside the database we can think of it, for this chapter, as being logically outside of the database.

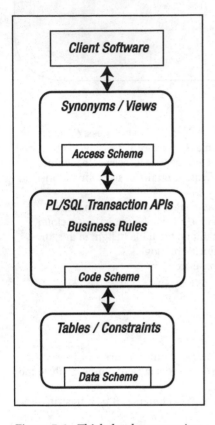

Figure 5-1. *Thick database overview*

Data Schema: The Data Schema contains the data. Ideally, this schema should be locked so that no human can log on as the schema user and directly manipulate the data and the structure. APEX itself uses this technique to protect the APEX_500000 schema.

Code Schema: The Code Schema is responsible for maintaining the data in the Data Schema. The Code Schema contains PL/SQL routines that handle all of the Create, Retrieve, Update, and Delete (CRUD) SQL statements that are applied against the data tables. In addition, these routines are in charge of defining the transaction scope, which is why they are often called a Transaction Application Program Interface (XAPI). For example, there might be a routine named CREATE_SOMETHING. The "something" is actually described by data in more than one table. The CREATE_SOMETHING routine must issue multiple SQL statements and then commit the work if all goes well or roll back the work if an error occurs. In addition, the code must enforce the business rules that are associated with the "something".

Do not confuse an XAPI with a Table Application Program Interface (TAPI). A TAPI is a set of PL/SQL routines that maintain a single table. These routines are often used by an XAPI as "helper" functions and they are rarely exposed as public routines; an exception could be made when the underlying table is a simple lookup table that has no dependencies. TAPIs will not contain COMMIT or ROLLBACK statements; those statements belong to the XAPI that is responsible for a complete transaction.

Access Schema: The Access Schema is a schema that the client software can see. For security reasons, the client software should only see the database objects for which it is responsible and be granted only the database privileges that are required to get its work done. This type of schema is often almost empty, containing nothing but views and synonyms that point to the XAPI routines.

The thick database architecture wraps a hard, protective shell around the data. This protective shell does the following:

- *Maximizes the probability of correct data.* The data manipulation routines are in one place; therefore, there is a single source of truth when the business rules are applied. Testing resources are concentrated on one set of code instead of being scattered over several client software programs that may or may not be well crafted. Bear in mind that the business rules can also be and should be validated in the browser or in the client software. The main purpose of these client-side software validations is to enhance the user experience; however, they should not be relied on to be the primary protectors of the data.

- *Maximizes the probability of good performance.* Since both the data and the logic reside in the same database and server, there is no network latency slowing things down. In addition, PL/SQL is an extremely efficient and rock-solid tool.

- *Maximizes the probability of a secure environment.* The Access Schema exposes a minimum of database detail; therefore, the potential hacker attack surface is minimized.

This summary of the thick database architecture is a "bare bones" treatment of the subject. In reality, large systems can be sub-divided into many data, code, and Access Schemas that are tailored to the tasks at hand. More importantly, there can be many client software programs that will be used to update the data; these range from APEX, Oracle Forms, .NET, Java, and even good old SQL*Plus. Never assume your APEX application is the only tool that will be updating your data.

Before building or enhancing a large cloud or enterprise system, it is a good idea to have the "thick database" chat with all of the teams that will be affected; finding the optimal setup in this area can dramatically increase quality and reduce the overall cost of the system. And remember, the database design, if done well, will most probably outlive all of the client software programs by many years, even decades.

APEX in a Thick Database

How does APEX fit into the thick database paradigm? Should it? If so, why? Let's mull over these questions and let you, the reader, decide what is optimal for your situation.

First, lets look at the architecture that is used by default by many APEX shops. Figure 5-2 illustrates the common APEX practice of putting both data tables and logic into one APEX parsing schema that is used by many APEX applications.

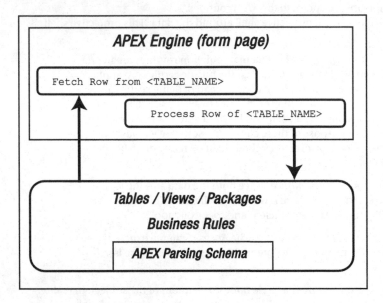

Figure 5-2. *APEX common default data architecture*

The main advantage of doing this is convenience. This strategy allows APEX developers to use the declarative wizards to bind reports and data entry forms directly to the base tables. This is where APEX's rapid application development (RAD) feature shines; development using this scenario can be extremely fast.

The main disadvantage of doing this is a lack of control over the business rules. In this case, APEX developers must rely on APEX validations to enforce the business rules. This, of course, leaves the database vulnerable to bad data being inserted by other clients that have no business rule enforcement or that have a different version of the business rules. The cost of cleaning up a garbage data insert or update can easily cancel out the savings that were gained by a fast, low-cost APEX development effort. Another disadvantage is related to security; this architecture exposes much more database functionality to potential hackers than an isolated Access Schema.

It is possible, using the default APEX parsing schema scenario, to enforce the business rules on the database server by using triggers that are attached to each table. Warning! This is probably not a good idea. Refer to an article by Tom Kyte, "The Trouble with Triggers," in the September/October 2008 issue of *Oracle Magazine* (http://www.oracle.com/technetwork/testcontent/o58asktom-101055.html). This article clearly articulates two primary reasons for avoiding complex triggers—long-term maintenance headaches and very subtle implementation issues. The article is almost ten years old but it is still valid and these issues should be considered in any business rule design discussion.

Triggers can, of course, be safely used for simple tasks like generating primary key and audit values.

There are two important points that are associated with this scenario:

- The COMMIT and ROLLBACK logic is controlled by the APEX engine.

- Only one data source can be manipulated by the declarative FETCH ROW and PROCESS ROW processes.

The former point tends to force developers to enforce business rules through APEX validations.

The latter point has been a sore point with end users who use APEX 5.0 and the earlier versions. Many of them are accustomed to using client/server applications like Oracle Forms, which has widgets that update multiple data sources on a single page. This point is greatly mitigated by the Interactive Grid that has been introduced in APEX 5.1. Two or more Interactive Grids can coexist on a single page, as shown in Figure 5-3. The Save buttons that are associated with the individual Interactive Grid regions update their associated grid through an AJAX call. The Save button in the upper-right corner performs a full page submit. In this case, all Interactive Grids on a page are saved and, if an error occurs, the ROLLBACK affects them all.

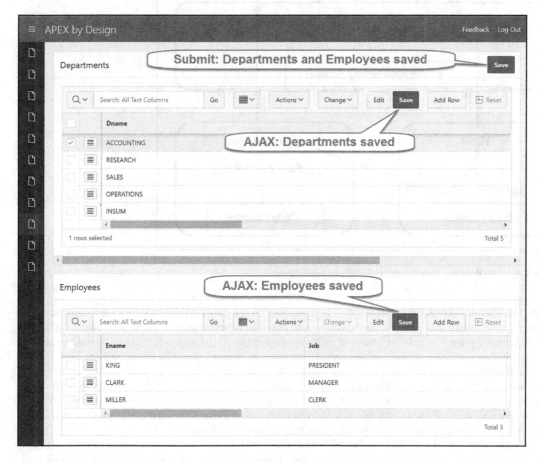

Figure 5-3. *APEX Interactive Grids support multiple data sources on one page*

Another interesting feature of Interactive Grids is their ability to be linked together in Master/Detail/Detail relationships to an arbitrary depth. This feature significantly affects our approach to designing APEX data entry forms.

Now let's look at how APEX can utilize the concepts found in the thick database paradigm. Figure 5-4 outlines the architecture.

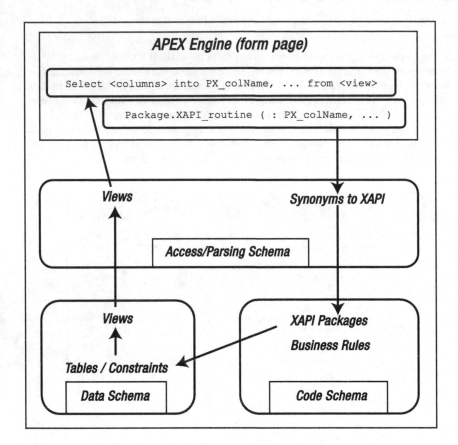

Figure 5-4. *APEX fitting into the thick database paradigm*

The Data Schema contains the tables that, in turn, contain the data and constraints. Constraints are an effective mechanism that protects your data from all client changes no matter where they originate. The tables, in turn, are joined into views. The read-only views are exposed through select grants to the Access Schema.

The Access Schema, in this case, is also the application's parsing schema. The views in the Access Schema are used directly by the APEX application to populate reports, charts, and the default values in data entry forms. In this architecture, data entry forms cannot use the declarative FETCH ROW process to automatically populate the data entry items; it must be replaced by a hand-coded PL/SQL process that contains SELECT INTO statements that copy the data into the individual page items.

In the APEX engine, the declarative PROCESS ROW process is replaced by a hand-coded PL/SQL process that contains a call to an XAPI routine that updates the database. The PL/SQL processes can be invoked by either a full page submit or an AJAX call. The form item values are passed as parameters to the XAPI routines. The XAPI routines contain the business logic that is associated with the individual business transactions. When a transaction completes with no exception, then the data from the page items is inserted or updated in the appropriate tables. The new data conforms to the business rules that were in place at the time of the change.

The following two thick database paradigm points are in direct contrast to the default APEX scenario:

- The COMMIT and ROLLBACK logic is controlled by the XAPI routines.

- Multiple data sources can be manipulated by the XAPI routines.

This strategy gives the developer much greater control over database data changes.

The declarative nature of APEX is an attractive feature that can save developers much time. Can this feature be woven into the thick database paradigm? The answer is "sort of". Figure 5-5 shows a simple architecture that might work. This scenario adds updateable views to the APEX parsing schema. The updateable views look like tables to the declarative APEX framework; therefore APEX's declarative functionality comes into full play. The downsides are related to security and complexity. From a security perspective, the updatable views give a hacker a slightly larger attack surface with which to work. From a complexity perspective, the updatable views and the XAPI routines give developers two ways to change data instead of one; this might be an issue in large teams that employ interns and junior developers.

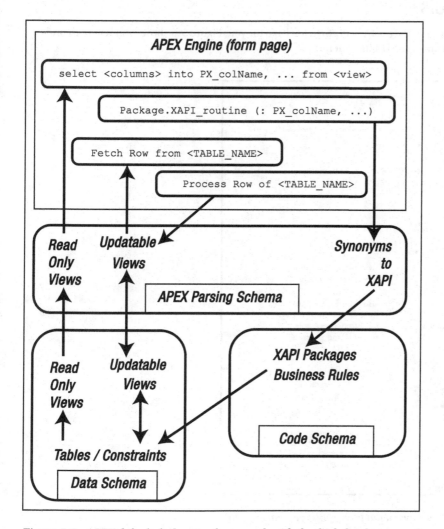

Figure 5-5. APEX default declarative framework with the thick database paradigm

DEV vs. TEST and PROD Environments

Another thing to think about is whether or not you want the development environment to mimic the test and production environments.

If the development environment mimics the test and production environments by using the thick database paradigm, developers will find it tedious to constantly deal with grants as they add and delete tables during the initial stages of development.

On the other hand, if the developers ignore the thick database paradigm in development to speed up development, then they will pay a price when moving a new version from development to test. In this case, there will be additional work during testing to get the grants set up correctly.

The development and testing teams will need to discuss this and optimize the setup for the enterprise's particular case.

TAPI Helper Tools

APEX contains a utility that generates a TAPI PL/SQL package for you. Figure 5-6 shows you where to find this tool in SQL Workshop under the Utilities menu.

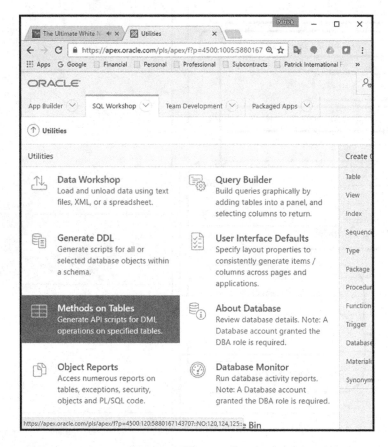

Figure 5-6. *SQL Workshop utility: Methods on Tables generates a TAPI*

Figure 5-7 illustrates that you can create a TAPI package on up to ten tables in your parsing schema, and Figure 5-8 lists the four public methods that are exposed by default.

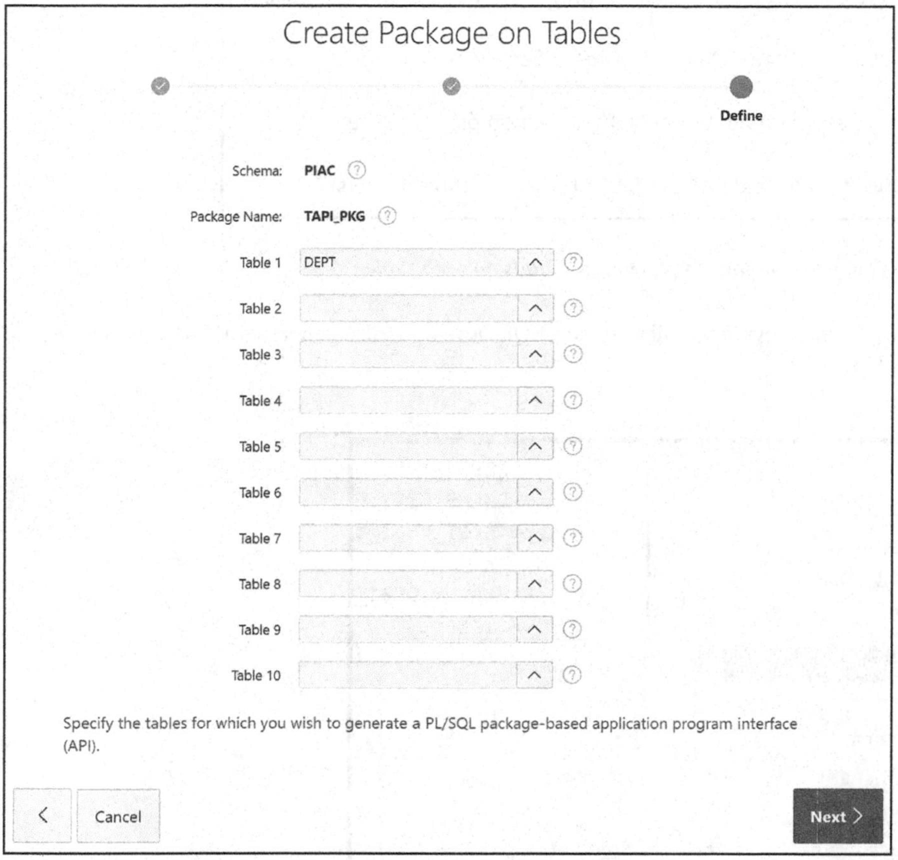

Figure 5-7. APEX TAPI generation tool creates a package on up to ten tables

Subprogram	Description
ins_dept	use to insert data into **DEPT**, primary key needs to be supplied
upd_dept	use to update data in **DEPT** identified by primary key(s)
del_dept	use to delete data from **DEPT** based on primary key(s)
get_dept	use to retieve data from **DEPT** based on primary key(s)

Figure 5-8. *APEX TAPI generation tool creates four methods on each table*

There are other tools that provide a similar service. SQL Developer also generates a TAPI on a single table, as illustrated in Figure 5-9.

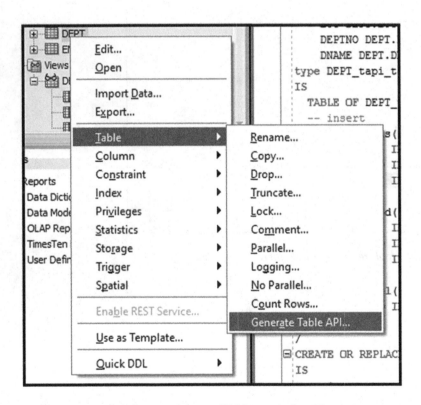

Figure 5-9. *SQL Developer generates a TAPI on a single table*

The TAPI generation tools can save you quite a bit of typing; however, they generate only very basic code. Developers need to enhance the code to bring it up to their production standards by adding instrumentation, table specific business logic, and exception handling. Of course, developers must be careful when the table changes; they must decide whether to regenerate the TAPI and re-apply the customizations or add the new columns to the already generated code.

TAPI routines can be used directly or as helper routines inside a larger XAPI context.

- *Direct TAPI usage*: A single table TAPI can be used directly by the client code when the table does not contain data dependencies on other tables. In other words, data changes are made in the one table and changes to other tables are not required.

- *TAPIs inside an XAPI*: Transactions in a large data model often require changes to multiple tables. In this case, the TAPI routines are called from the XAPI routine as private "helper" routines.

Some organizations develop their own custom TAPI code generators. In this case, the developers have needs that are not met by the current commercial or open source TAPI generators. This course of action can add a valuable veneer of consistency on top of a large and complicated data model. Two blogs and an open source project speak to this topic and contain valuable insights for developers who want to pursue this strategy. The links are:

- *thatjeffsmith.com*: Jeff Smith is currently the product manager for Oracle SQL Developer. He has a lot of practical experience with the current offerings in the PL/SQL code generation space, plus a lot of insights into past code generators like Oracle Designer. Search his blog for "Table APIs" and similar strings.

- *stevenfeuersteinonplsql.blogspot.ca*: Steven Feuerstein is a prolific author, speaker, and blogger on Oracle PL/SQL. Searching his blog for "code generator" will give you lots of food for thought.

- *github.com/osalvador/tapiGen2*: The tapiGen2 project was created in 2015 by Oscar Salvador Magallanes. It was based on an earlier open source project, tapiGen by Dan McGhan. This tool allows developers to create code templates; it also includes LOGGER (another open source project on GitHub) code for exception handling.

Large cloud and enterprise software environments often involve hundreds and even thousands of tables. TAPI code generation should be strongly considered and researched so that the systems are built to be consistent, performant, and secure.

Optimistic Locking

The web is a stateless environment. This means that lost update protection is normally accomplished by using an optimistic record locking strategy. Let's define a few terms to set the stage for this discussion.

- *Lost update*: Consider a scenario where two end users want to edit the same table row in a database. User one takes a copy of the record and loads it into an update form in the client software. User two takes a copy of the same record, completes the update task, and saves the updated record. Then, at a later time, user one updates the record and overwrites user two's changes. User two's changes are a "lost update". Audit tables, if they exist, can be used to correct this issue, but only after the loss has been discovered and a considerable amount of time has been expended. This is not a good situation.

- *Pessimistic locking*: Client/server applications prevent lost updates by physically locking the record when user one copies the record into the update form. User two cannot access the record until user one releases the lock by either cancelling or committing the update process. In this case, a lost update is impossible. Pessimistic locking works because a client maintains a permanent connection to the database and only releases the lock when the application completes its work with the record.

- *Optimistic locking*: A web application, like APEX, must not physically lock a record due to the fact that there is no guarantee that the application will reconnect to the database to unlock the record. In this case, the concept of version is applied to the record. When a record is copied into an update form, a record version is computed and sent along with the data. APEX computes a checksum value for this purpose. When the updated page is submitted, the update process recomputes the checksum value. If the two checksum values are the same, then the routine knows that the record has not changed since the record was copied into the application. If the checksum values are different, then the routine knows that another user or process has updated the record; in this case, the update is aborted and a message is shown to the user.

Optimistic locking is the default behavior for the declarative PROCESS ROW of <table name> process. You cannot turn this feature off as it is part of the APEX engine.

Now what do developers need to do when they code their own database update PL/SQL routines? Should they add optimistic locking or ignore it? There is a cost associated with adding optimistic locking to the update code; the cost is associated with performance and code complexity. Another consideration is the probability of two users or processes wanting to update a single record at the same time. Developers need to consider the cost and performance overhead of adding optimistic locking to possibly hundreds of update routines and thousands of update transactions versus the benefit of avoiding one lost transaction in possibly several million transactions; of course, the value of that one individual transaction must also be considered. Banks, for example, would never tolerate even one lost transaction. Saving a single low value transaction, on the other hand, might not be worth the effort or performance cost. This topic is fodder for an interesting design meeting among developers and the persons who are in charge of risk analysis.

Listing 5-1 contains the TAPI update procedure that is generated by the APEX utility; it also contains the routine that calculates the checksum value for optimistic locking. The P_MD5 parameter refers to the checksum value. The code adds a bit of perspective to this discussion with regard to the added complexity of the code.

Listing 5-1. TAPI Update Procedure Generated by APEX

```
-----------------------------------------------------------------
-- update procedure for table "DEPT"
   procedure "UPD_DEPT" (
      "P_DEPTNO" in number,
      "P_DNAME"    in varchar2                  default null,
      "P_LOC"      in varchar2                  default null,
      "P_MD5"      in varchar2                  default null
   ) is

      "L_MD5" varchar2(32767) := null;

   begin

      if "P_MD5" is not null then
         for c1 in (
            select * from "DEPT"
            where "DEPTNO" = "P_DEPTNO" FOR UPDATE
         ) loop
```

```
        "L_MD5" := "BUILD_DEPT_MD5"(
          c1."DEPTNO",
          c1."DNAME",
          c1."LOC"
        );

      end loop;

    end if;

    if ("P_MD5" is null) or ("L_MD5" = "P_MD5") then
      update "DEPT" set
        "DEPTNO"      = "P_DEPTNO",
        "DNAME"       = "P_DNAME",
        "LOC"         = "P_LOC"
      where "DEPTNO" = "P_DEPTNO";
    else
      raise_application_error (-20001,'Current version of data in database has changed
      since user initiated update process. current checksum = "'||"L_MD5"||'"', item
      checksum = "'||"P_MD5"||'".');
    end if;

  end "UPD_DEPT";

----------------------------------------------------------------
-- build MD5 function for table "DEPT"
  function "BUILD_DEPT_MD5" (
    "P_DEPTNO" in number,
    "P_DNAME"    in varchar2                           default null,
    "P_LOC"      in varchar2                           default null
  ) return varchar2 is

  begin

    return apex_util.get_hash(apex_t_varchar2(
      "P_DNAME",
      "P_LOC" ));

  end "BUILD_DEPT_MD5";
```

Figure 5-10 shows what optimistic locking looks like in the APEX debug page. You can see that there are two SQL statements that are issued by the declarative PROCESS ROW of <table name> process. The first statement is the SELECT statement that calculates the checksum value. The second statement is the UPDATE statement that does the work of updating the database. It is interesting to note that, in this specific case, the statement that calculates the checksum value takes a bit longer than the statement that updates the database. This experiment was repeated a number of times on the apex.oralce.com site using APEX 5.1 and this trend appeared to be consistent where the checksum computation consumed, on average, 61% of the total transaction time. Before your team has the optimistic locking chat, you should check the explicit performance numbers in your specific environment.

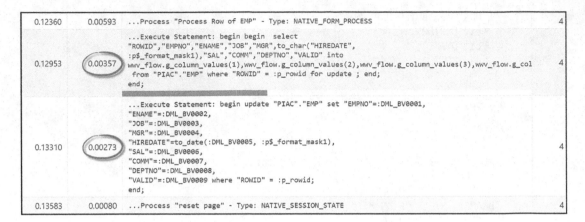

Figure 5-10. Performance cost of optimistic locking

Summary

Making sure that the data in an enterprise database is clean is a prime directive for database developers. Exploiting the thick database paradigm is arguably the best way to ensure data integrity with the side benefits of good performance and security. APEX can be configured so that it takes advantage of the thick database paradigm; this strategy should be strongly considered by the APEX design team when moving from a departmental development environment to a large cloud and enterprise environment. The design discussions should also touch on the topics of the development versus test/production setups, TAPI helper tools, and optimistic locking. These design discussions must include the developer, DBA, infrastructure, and security stakeholders.

CHAPTER 6

∎ ∎ ∎

Cookie Applications

Divide and conquer. This saying, in a software context, means that one's chances for success can increase when you take a large, complex application, and break it down into bite-sized pieces. APEX makes this strategy relatively easy by enabling individual APEX applications to communicate with one another by sharing a single browser cookie. A single login application opens the door to running multiple specialized APEX applications without the need to log in multiple times. This chapter explores this strategy in more detail.

APEX Cookie Application Architecture

The APEX development environment is a good example of linking cookie applications together. There are five marquee APEX development applications:

- Application Builder (application ID = 4000)
- SQL Workshop (application ID = 4500)
- Team Development (application ID = 4800)
- Packaged Applications (application ID = 4750)
- Administration (application ID = 4350)

© Patrick Cimolini 2017

P. Cimolini, *Oracle Application Express by Design*, https://doi.org/10.1007/978-1-4842-2427-4_6

You can see proof of this architecture by observing how the application ID changes in the APEX URL as you click into each of the APEX development areas (see Figure 6-1). The Administration application is found under the administration drop-down menu in the menu bar.

Figure 6-1. *APEX development environment consists of several separate applications*

There are a number of advantages to splitting up a large application into smaller, special-purpose applications. It may be easier to manage smaller applications that maintain specific sub-systems; individual teams can concentrate on their business area of expertise without fear of accidentally breaking an unrelated area. Authorization schemes can be simplified where a single authorization scheme can be applied to a single small application instead of to many individual navigation links, pages, and processes that reside in a large multi-module application. The small applications can each have their own parsing schema that contains only the data objects that it needs; this can enhance security. Maintenance programming is much less risky and it is easier for maintenance programmers to find their way around in a small application. Promoting a single small application from development to test and production requires potentially a lot less effort than promoting a single large application; this might be an issue in regulated industries that require full regression testing and quality assurance documentation when a new version is promoted.

Figure 6-2 shows one potential way that cookie applications could be organized. You will, I am sure, think of other strategies that will be better suited to your situation. Let's explore the figure to see how it is hooked up in detail.

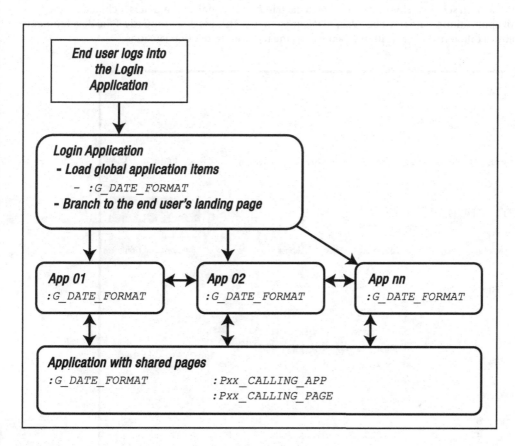

Figure 6-2. *One way of organizing cookie applications*

Cookie Name Attribute

All of the applications that work together share common attributes. The most important attribute is the shared cookie name shown in Figure 6-3. The Cookie Name attribute is associated with an application's current authentication scheme. This attribute is set in each individual application that is included in the linked suite of applications. Care must be taken to ensure that the attribute is set properly if the development version employs a different authentication scheme from the test and production versions.

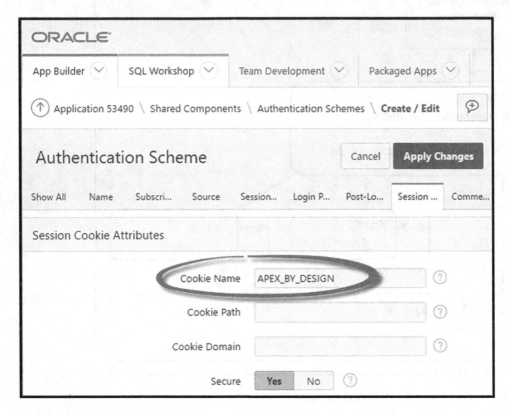

Figure 6-3. *The cookie name is set in an application's current authentication scheme*

The Cookie Name attribute enables all of the related applications on a user's computer to use a single cookie environment. This is the trick that enables users to glide effortlessly between the separate applications without the need to authenticate when moving between applications.

Global Application Items

It is a common practice to load handy bits of data into application items for easy reference throughout an application. You might want to look up things like a user's full name, e-mail address, phone number, etc. In a cookie application environment, you will want these global application items to be available to all the cookie applications. This is achieved by:

- Creating the shared application items in each cookie application.

- Setting the application's Scope attribute to Global in each cookie application.

- Loading the appropriate values into the global application items once immediately after the user logs in.

Figure 6-4 illustrates the Scope attribute that is associated with every application item.

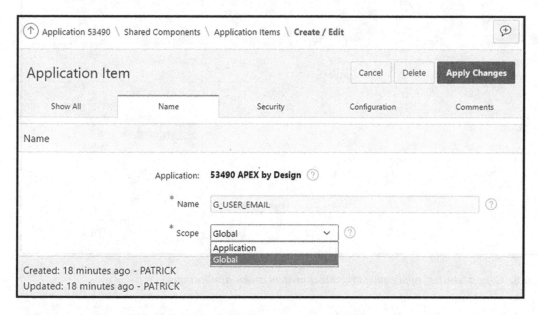

Figure 6-4. *Set the Scope attribute to Global so it is shared among all cookie apps*

You should spend some design time thinking about exactly what global application items that you need for a large project. This step might not be critical when you only have two or three cookie applications because adding a new global application item is a relatively trivial task. On the other hand, if you anticipate that the number of cookie applications will be large, you will want to discuss the following points:

- *Define the full list of global application items together with an easy-to-use naming convention before serious application development begins.* You may want the naming convention to indicate the scope of an application item; use a "G_" prefix for application items that are shared by cookie applications and use an "A_" prefix for applications items that are local to a single application.

- *Consider creating a starter application (see Figure 6-5) that contains your list of application items and create new cookie applications as a copy of this starter application.* This strategy will save time when you create a new cookie application because all of the basic plumbing, like the authentication scheme, will be in place. This is also a great way to add consistency to your environment because all cookie applications are built on the same footing.

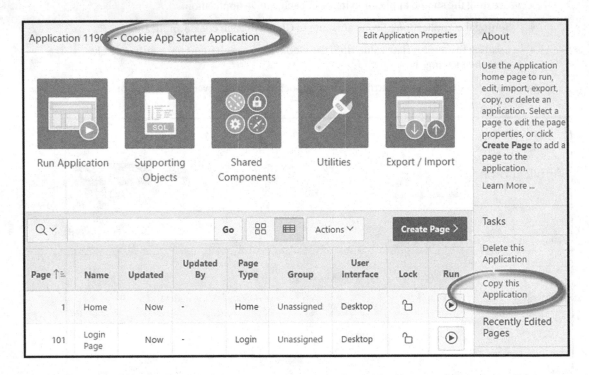

Figure 6-5. *Copy a "starter" application to create consistent cookie applications*

- *Consider creating a master shared component application that links its shared components to the starter application through APEX's subscription mechanism.* When the cookie applications are created as a copy of the starter application, the created cookie applications inherit the subscriptions to the master shared component application. This setup puts a master copy of your shared components into a single place where they are maintained. When a master shared component is changed, the new version can either be pushed out to all of the cookie applications at one time or pulled into the cookie application one at a time. The push strategy works well for very low-risk changes while the pull strategy must be employed for higher-risk changes that require rigorous testing before being deployed out to production.

Figure 6-6 summarizes the cookie application architecture that employs both a starter and a master shared component application. Figures 6-7 and 6-8 are screenshots illustrating the subtle differences between a master shared component and a subscriber version of the same shared component. Now you might think that making a physical copy of a shared component in every cookie application is rather awkward; you are correct, but as of APEX 5.1 this is how shared components work.

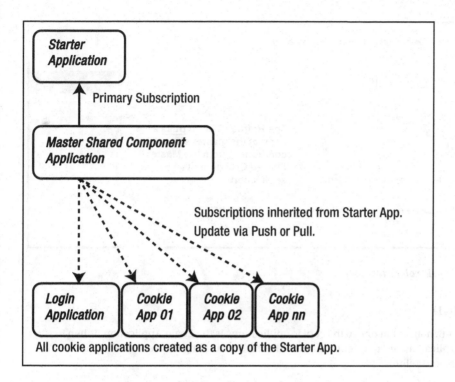

Figure 6-6. Subscription architecture

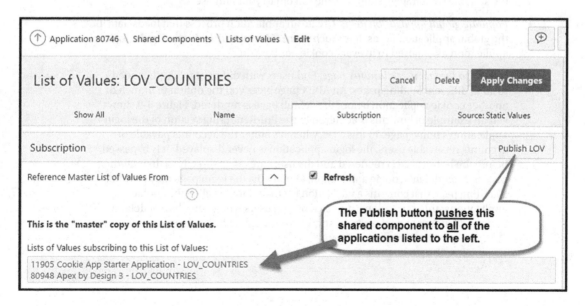

Figure 6-7. The master side of a subscription

Figure 6-8. *The subscriber side of a subscription*

Login Application

Looking back to Figure 6-6, notice that one of the cookie applications is the Login Application. When constructing a cookie application environment, you should consider building this very small application. It has several primary responsibilities:

- *Authentication*: It is used as the single point of entry into the cookie application environment. This means that all of your end users are given a single URL to access the system. This strategy simplifies the roll out to your end users.

- *Populate global application items*: Create an application process that loads data into the global application items. It is much more efficient to do this once in the login application as opposed to in every cookie application.

- *Branch to the end user's landing page*: End users with different roles often need to go to different landing pages. An APEX page gives you the option to branch to another cookie application before the default page is rendered. Figure 6-9 shows you an example of how this is achieved in the Pre-Rendering section of the login application's home page. In this case, when it's either the accounts payable or accounts receivable users, the login application is never displayed. It is bypassed before the home page is rendered and the users are taken directly to their landing page in their default cookie application. Optionally, the login page may contain a landing page that contains a navigation list that points to all of the cookie applications; this navigation list is used by end users who do not have a default or preferred landing page. An administration user might fall into this category.

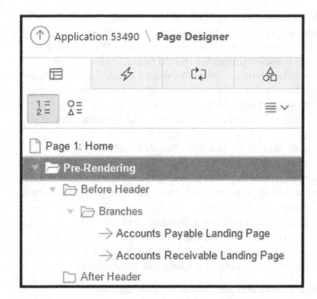

Figure 6-9. *Login application branches to default landing cookie applications*

Sharing Regions and Pages Among Cookie Apps

In a large application environment that is split into many separate cookie applications, it is quite probable that you will find instances of regions and pages that you want to reuse. Code reuse is an efficient thing to do since it enforces consistency and defines a "single source of the truth" for a component.

Sharing Regions

Regions can be shared across multiple applications by creating region plug-ins. Creating plug-ins is beyond the scope of this book; however, I refer you to the book, *Expert Oracle Application Express Plugins*, by Martin D'Souza (Apress).

Sharing Pages

Sharing pages across multiple cookie applications is relatively simple to do technically because it is easy to construct a URL that navigates to an APEX page in the same or a different application; however, there are some design issues that should be considered.

Refer back to Figure 6-2 and notice that it suggests building a separate application that contains pages that are shared among the cookie applications. Programmers who use this design strategy know explicitly that changes to a page in the shared application will affect many applications; therefore, they will take care to find out which applications share the page to make sure that the changes are compatible with all of the affected applications. An alternative strategy is to let the cookie applications "borrow" pages from their siblings; this can be dangerous because programmers might not be aware that a given page is in fact a shared page and they could make changes that would inadvertently affect other applications.

Shared pages require some thought when considering navigation. When end users complete their work on a shared page, they most probably want to return to the page from where they called the shared page. This is easily accomplished by adding two hidden items to the shared page, Pxx_CALLING_APP and Pxx_CALLING_PAGE where xx is the page number that is associated with the shared page. A calling page would set these the values of these hidden items in the branch that invokes the shared page. The shared page uses these values to branch back to the calling page. These hidden items would contain the application alias and page alias that are associated with calling application and page. Using the aliases makes the URL easier to read and makes it more robust in cases where the application IDs change between the development, test, and production environments.

The Cancel button on a shared page will most probably use the Pxx_CALLING_APP and Pxx_CALLING_PAGE hidden items by default. In many cases, the branch after processing will also use the hidden items to get back to the calling pages; however, in some cases the user of the code might not want to automatically return to the calling page. In this case, you may need to add appropriate navigation lists that are dependent on the end user's role and that are controlled by an authorization scheme.

Another important consideration is the shared application's parsing schema. If all of the cookie applications share the same parsing schema, then there is no problem; the shared application simply uses the shared parsing schema. If each cookie application accesses its own parsing schema that is tailored to the cookie application's explicit needs, then the shared application's parsing schema will need either:

- The appropriate grants from the parsing schemas that are involved in the common transactions
- The appropriate grants from the underlying data schema

In both cases, this situation might raise issues related to security and complexity; these topics must be evaluated during design discussions.

Parameters That Will Never Change

I am always a bit nervous and skeptical when I hear the phrase, "this will never change". In our software world, this attitude can lead to software that is littered with unmaintainable literal strings and magic numbers. When parameters "that will never change" actually change, the following code scenario can be insidiously difficult to refactor:

```
doSomethingProcedure( '2' ) ;
doSomethingElseProcedure( '2' ) ;
```

If the first '2' refers to a status, for example, and the second to a priority, then you are potentially faced with a high-risk and high-cost refactoring project when one of the values changes to '42'.

This section outlines some of the design choices that you can make in an APEX context that will convert this code to something much safer, like the following:

```
doSomethingProcedure( :G_STATUS_NORMAL ) ;
doSomethingElseProcedure( :G_PRIORITY_HIGH ) ;
```

This strategy enables the change from '2' to '42' to be done in only one place. No other code needs to be touched.

One of the most common excuses for hard-coding a string like '2' is "we don't have time" to define the global constants. This is ironic because, in a large cloud and enterprise application, the hard-coded '2' will probably cost the team much more development time than the soft-coded global constant. This situation is due to the following facts:

- The meaning of '2' must be explained to every new developer when they join the project.

- The meaning of '2' is confusing when it is used in two contexts, status and priority, for example. This will cause subtle bugs that will add to testing and debugging time.

- Over time, the meaning of '2' will be forgotten. This can cost a considerable amount of time when a developer is looking for a bug and must determine if the '2' is related to the bug or not by reading code to determine how '2' is used.

The bottom line here is that in large systems, defining and populating a global constant or variable will actually save you a considerable amount of time when compared to the so-called expedient hard-coded literals. In fact, this very strategy is adopted by the developers at Oracle Corporation, who write the many PL/SQL packages that are included with the database and underlying advanced functionality such as APEX.

You might wonder why a parameter "that will never change" will be changed. There are many reasons; one example could be that your standard date format must change when your company merges with a bigger foreign company. This might happen only once or twice in a lifetime, but when it does, it can be costly if the computer systems that must be merged are full of literal date format strings.

Substitution Strings

APEX makes it exceptionally quick and easy to define global constants within a single application. This feature is called *Substitutions* and it is found in the Edit Application Definition area (see Figure 6-10).

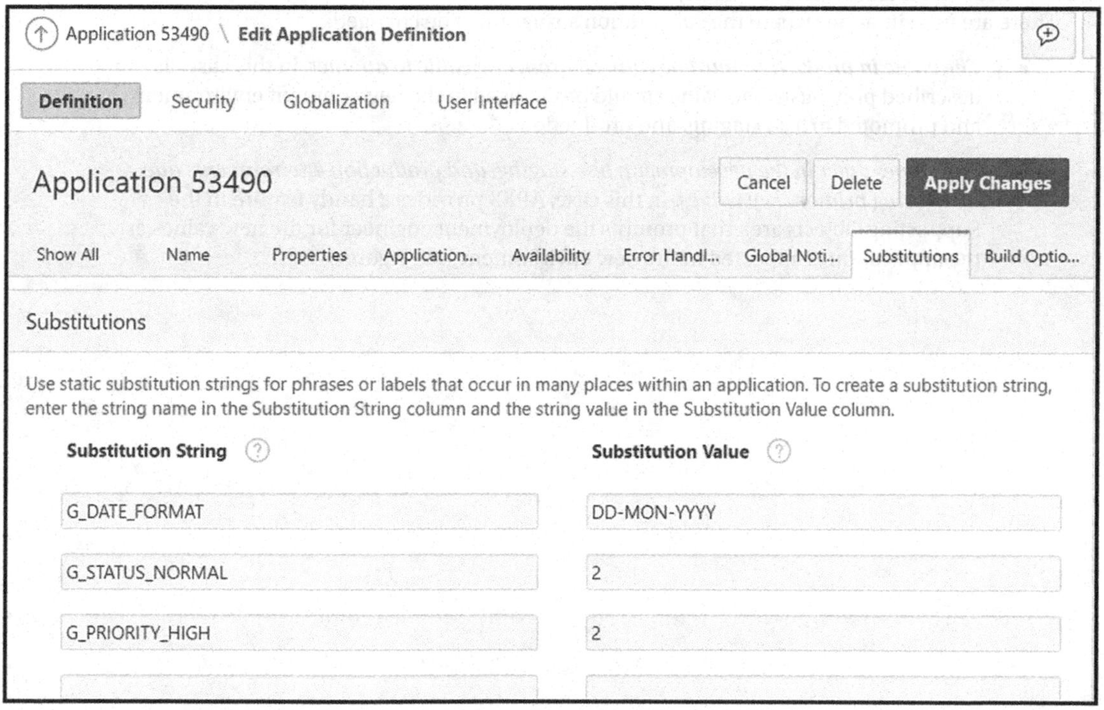

Figure 6-10. *APEX Substitutions*

It is clear that the Substitution Strings and Substitution Values can be entered extremely quickly. Referencing these values is done by using the standard APEX syntax options:

```
:G_DATE_FORMAT
&G_DATE_FORMAT.
V('G_DATE_FORMAT')
```

This feature works well for single applications where deployment to the test and production environment does not involve a lot of overhead.

This feature does not work well in larger environments where the overall system may be made up of a number of related but separate APEX cookie applications and the deployment of applications must go through a formal quality assurance process. In this case, the drawbacks of this scenario are:

- A simple change of '2' to '42' to a substitution string, even if no other changes are made, requires the entire application to be deployed to test and production.

- When the system is made up of multiple APEX cookie applications that contain an identical set of substitution strings, then all of the applications must be deployed when the value of a substitution string changes.

Note that application deployment can be avoided if the APEX developer tool is enabled in the production environment so that the change can be made directly in the production application. In this case, care must be taken to ensure that the change is also reflected in the development environment. In general, enabling the developer tool in production is frowned upon, as it is tempting to slip in other seemingly trivial changes that the end users have requested. This is the proverbial "slippery slope". Enabling the developer tool in production is also a serious security issue.

There are two situations where the substitution strings must be changed:

- *The value in production must be changed from one value to another.* In this case, as described previously, the value should be changed in the development environment and promoted to test, staging, and production.

- *The values differ in the development, test, staging, and production environments due to differing primary key values.* In this case, APEX provides a handy feature in the Supporting Objects area that prompts the deployment engineer for the new values as the application is imported in the new environment (see Figure 6-11).

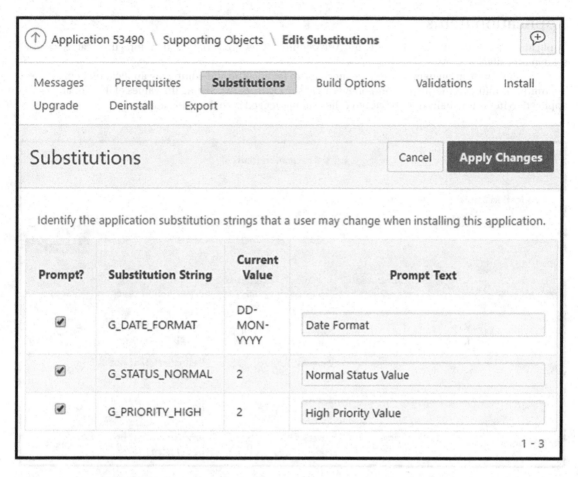

Figure 6-11. *Supporting objects prompt for new substitution values*

While substitution stings are easy and quick to set up, I know of several senior APEX developers who recommend that they not be used in larger APEX systems. Instead, they prefer using the dynamic techniques that are described in the following sections.

Note that substitution strings are in fact, global constants; their values cannot be changed dynamically in PL/SQL code or through the APEX URL.

Application Items

Application items are global variables in the APEX context. They are variables; therefore, their values can be set dynamically.

Creating application items is easy; the mechanism for creating and editing the application item definitions is found in the shared components area (see Figure 6-12). Setting the values of the global application items is usually done once, after the user has logged in to the application.

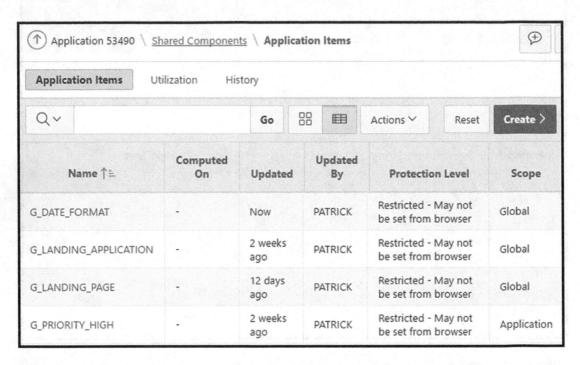

Figure 6-12. Application items are created and edited in shared components

Remember that application items are global variables; however, they are often used as global constants whose values must never change after they are initially set. If you have a mix of application items that are used as constants and application items that are used as variables, then you should probably consider using a naming convention so that the developers can easily see the difference in the code to prevent accidental changes to an application item that is used as a constant. For example, "GC_" for global constant and "GV_" for global variable prefixes could be used in this case.

Parameter Table

Initializing global application items is a straightforward thing to do. You can store the persistent values in any number of convenient formats. A two column name-value parameter table might be the easiest option in an Oracle context. Other options to consider are text files that are stored on the web server in JSON, XML, or CSV formats.

No matter which format you prefer, they all have the following characteristics:

- *Formatted as name-value pairs.*

- *Data is loaded either when a new APEX session is created or just after a user has logged in.* The new APEX session option is used for situations where an end user accesses an application via a public page and the parameters are independent from any single user. Parameters that depend on the end user's ID must, of course, be set after the user logs in.

- *Values are maintained through a very simple administration utility that is accessed very infrequently.* This administration utility is placed under the control of the configuration team, who can adjust these values directly in the production environment when necessary after the change has been tested in one of the non-production environments that mirrors the production environment.

PL/SQL Constant Package

Storing the "parameters that will never change" in global APEX application items is not the only option. You could consider storing them in a PL/SQL package that makes the values available through functions that can, like application items, be accessed in both SQL and PL/SQL contexts.

The PL/SQL functions will execute each time a parameter value is requested by code. This might seem inefficient; however, this can be done at a very low cost when you employ optimization techniques such as the PL/SQL function result cache. This Oracle feature allows you to look up a parameter value once from its underlying parameter table or file and then store it in an Oracle cache, where the next fetch is almost instantaneous.

The functions can retrieve their values in two ways:

- *As constants*: The values of the parameters could be hard-coded as constants. When the values change, which happens rarely, the PL/SQL constant package is recompiled with the new values.

- *Dynamically*: The values can be retrieved by reading them from a parameter table or other storage mechanism.

The PL/SQL constant package technique could be considered when your application environment is heavily dependent on many PL/SQL packages that contain very large sets of business rules. The PL/SQL only strategy makes the PL/SQL code independent from the APEX context and it does not impact the APEX GUI because the APEX GUI can easily access the PL/SQL functions to get the parameter values. If you employ the APEX application item technique, then you must pass the application items as parameters to the PL/SQL routines or instruct the PL/SQL routines to get the APEX application item values via the APEX "v" function. This latter technique might not be optimal when you consider the fact that the PL/SQL code may very well outlive the APEX GUI and will need to be refactored if and when the APEX GUI is replaced with a future GUI technology.

Designing Cookie Application Environments

In this discussion there are no tricky technical techniques. Coding an APEX cookie application environment is easy due to the declarative nature of APEX and the fact that APEX directly supports cookie applications.

So where is the difficulty? I would argue that the difficulty, in a large application environment, is in finding an optimal layout of cookie applications and their internal pages so that the business requirements are met in the most efficient overall manner. This means that intelligent trade-offs must be made when deciding how to explicitly place individual functionalities inside the overall architecture and how to link the functionalities so that the workflow is smooth and intuitive for potentially a large number of the user roles. In many cases, the "perfect" solution will not exist, the "practical" solution will consist of optimal trade-offs, which some of the participants will find somewhat painful. For example, some functionality might be duplicated on several "light" APEX pages, which will deeply offend some code purists, while other "heavy" APEX pages might be designed to support multiple user roles, which will deeply offend the people who love the "Keep it Simple, Stupid" (KISS) principle.

This type of analysis and design is not a quick and easy task. I have seen design rooms where the walls are covered with floor to ceiling whiteboards which, in turn, are covered with multi-colored line drawings and post-it notes, all of which can be erased, moved, and redrawn as ideas are considered, rejected, and reconsidered with new twists. This low-tech approach to design allows a number of team members to stand in the same room to debate and assess many design options and approaches. Out of this crucible, hopefully, a credible design will eventually emerge.

Summary

The APEX development environment makes it easy to divide a large application into small, special-purpose applications that share the same browser cookie; this means that all of the cookie applications can be accessed after the end user logs in one time. The architecture can be set up with a single login application that takes care of authenticating the end user, loading the global constants, and dispatching the end user to a preferred landing page. The individual cookie application can share a single set of global constants that makes common constant data easily available in all application contexts. The APEX subscription mechanism can be used to good effect by putting the definition of common shared components into a place that is the "single source of the truth"; changes can be pushed out to the cookie applications at one time or pulled into each cookie application on a one-at-a-time basis when they are ready to absorb the change.

The values of "parameters" that will never change can be coded statically in application-specific substitution strings or dynamically into global application items that are shared among all of the cookie applications. APEX provides all of the necessary declarative hooks to easily code the cookie application infrastructure. The hard work required is in finding the optimum placement of the business functionalities in the cookie application environment so that the end users have a smooth and intuitive experience; this design process requires much thought and discussion before coding begins.

CHAPTER 7

■ ■ ■

Authorization

Like many aspects of APEX, authorization schemes have been set up to be simple, declarative artifacts. A single APEX authorization scheme is much like a building brick. The act of laying a single brick, or even several bricks to make a simple structure like a raised garden flowerbed, is simple and easy to do; the design effort is trivial. Now the same simple construction element, the brick, can also be used as the fundamental building block for extremely large and complex structures like the Dome of Florence Cathedral in Italy, which is the largest brick dome in the world. Designing the cathedral was most definitely not a trivial effort. Like the cathedral, a large APEX cloud or enterprise computer system will need a major design effort before beginning to construct the system's complex interplay of permissions that relate people, roles, and responsibilities. Now let's discuss some of the design issues that are related to APEX authorization schemes.

The Need for Configuration

Large organizations evolve over time. The evolution often affects how people interact with their complex computer systems. Roles that people play expand, contract, merge, split, and retire as organizations respond to new market forces. Entirely new roles come into existence together with new technology and new business processes.

Adjusting software systems to accommodate role changes can be done as new versions of the software are released. Unfortunately, new software releases are scheduled on a relatively long release cycle that is often done on an annual or longer basis. Personnel changes occur on a much more frequent basis; therefore, it is reasonable to assume that building a dynamic model for linking people to roles and roles to responsibilities would be a cost-effective strategy. Indeed, existing large systems, like Oracle E-Business Suite (EBS), have done exactly that. APEX teams can learn a lot by looking at the permission architecture that EBS employs to manage permissions in production environments on a real-time basis.

Built-in Access Control Page

APEX offers a declarative wizard that builds an Access Control Page (see Figure 7-1). The wizard creates:

- Two tables in your parsing schema(s)

    - APEX_ACCESS_CONTROL

    - APEX_ACCESS_SETUP

- A single Access Control administration page that is local to your application

- Two static lists of values (LOVs) that are local to your application
    - APEX_APPLICATION_MODE
    - APEX_APPLICATION_PRIV
- Three authorization schemes that are local to your application
    - Access Control – Administrator
    - Access Control – Edit
    - Access Control – View

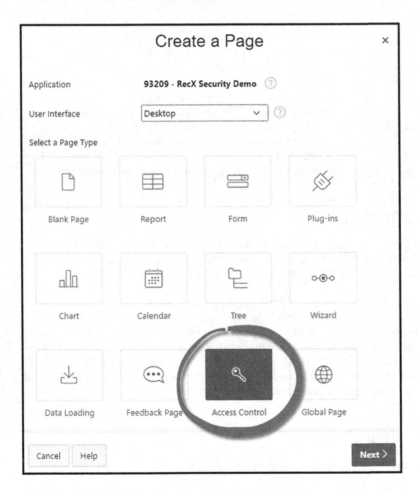

Figure 7-1. *APEX declarative Access Control Page wizard*

The two tables are created once per parsing schema. They manage access control for all of the applications that use the parsing schema. The APEX_ACCESS_CONTROL table links users to the three roles, while the APEX_ACCESS_SETUP table is used to store the Application Mode for each application that shares the common parsing schema. Figure 7-2 shows you the Access Control page for a single application; it gives you a good idea of how this component works.

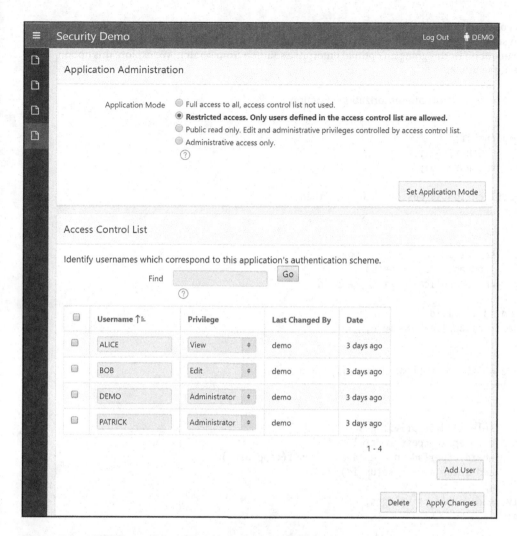

Figure 7-2. *APEX Access Control Page in a single application*

The Access Control Page wizard was added to APEX in the early days of the product. It is a sufficient solution for small application environments that have simplistic access control needs; however, it can be used as a learning tool or design template for a more sophisticated environment. Listing 7-1 is the PL/SQL function that is used for the Edit authorization scheme. The code does more than simply check the user's role; it also checks the application's authorization mode. As you can see, even in a very simple scenario, the authorization code is not trivial and there is a very real danger that the authorization code could explode in volume and complexity if the underlying design is not carefully considered before construction starts.

The built-in Access Control Page is a good example of a declarative component that should be replaced by a custom solution in a large cloud or enterprise environment. Yes, the Access Control component is quick and easy to build declaratively, but it has some drawbacks that are not easily remedied. First, it is a single application solution where each individual application contains its own list of users. This situation leads to a great deal of expensive redundancy for both the developers and the team that manages the production environment. Second, the solution supports only three roles. This is insufficient for larger environments where roles are not described simply by admin, edit, and view but by descriptions like accounts payable clerk I, accounts payable clerk II, etc.

A team could consider editing the existing Access Control page component so that it evolves into a design that supports a large distributed environment; however, in this case, I argue that a team would probably be better off by designing an optimal enterprise solution from scratch. We explore this option in the following sections.

Listing 7-1. Access Control Edit Authorization Function

```
declare
  l_setup_id number;
  l_mode     varchar2(50);
  l_priv     varchar2(50);
begin
  if apex_application.is_custom_auth_page then
    return true;
  end if;

  for c1 in (select id, application_mode
               from apex_access_setup
               where application_id = :app_id)
  loop
    l_setup_id := c1.id;
    l_mode := c1.application_mode;
  end loop;

  if (l_mode = 'ALL') or (l_mode is null) then
    return true;
  end if;

  for c1 in (select admin_privileges
               from apex_access_control
               where upper(admin_username) = upper(:app_user)
               and setup_id = l_setup_id)
  loop
    l_priv := c1.admin_privileges;
  end loop;

  if l_mode in ('RESTRICTED','PUBLIC_RESTRICTED') then
    if l_priv in ('EDIT','ADMIN') then
      return true;
    else
      return false;
    end if;
  elsif l_mode ='ADMIN_ONLY' then
    if l_priv = 'ADMIN' then
      return true;
    else
      return false;
    end if;
  else
    return false;
  end if;
  return false;
end;
```

Authorization Architecture

Minimizing the amount of code that is required to build a computer system is one of the goals of good architectural software design. Code is expensive both to build and to maintain; every line of code you write now is a future maintenance liability. Another architectural software goal is to build a configurable environment where end user change requests can be achieved by changing the production configuration instead of by changing code in the development environment. Making the production environment configurable enables a non-developer to make the change in a test environment, test the change, and then make the same change in the production environment. All this is done without changing the underlying application code.

Now let's look at how these principles are applied to the construction of a large APEX system using APEX authorization schemes.

Figure 7-3 illustrates the simplistic Entity Relationship Diagram (ERD) that many organizations use in practice. Users are given one or more roles and then the authorization schemes are built using these two entities. To support this architecture, developers quickly see the need to start adding multiple authorization schemes to support their user communities. For example, the APEX Access Control Page wizard builds three authorizations schemes—Administrator, Edit, and View. Now what happens when the end users identify the need for two "flavors" of the Edit authorization scheme? The answer is that developers must either add more logic to the existing authorization scheme or create an entirely new authorization scheme. As you can imagine, this strategy will soon lead to a chaotic and confusing authorization environment that is very expensive to maintain.

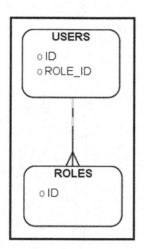

Figure 7-3. *Simplistic Authorization Entity Relationship Diagram (ERD)*

Developers tend to fall into this coding trap because:

- They inherit the simplistic user-role ERD from the authentication scheme

- Individual APEX authorization schemes are quick and easy to code

- No thought is given to managing future changes to authorization schemes in production

- Authorization schemes are added to applications late in the development cycle

- At the beginning of a project, developers underestimate the complexity of an enterprise authorization environment

71

Figure 7-4 is a more complete design that can allow the APEX authorization environment to be completely configurable in a production environment. Note that the illustrated architecture is only a suggestion here; your team might solve the problem using a different approach. The key take-away here is that you really need to design your authorization environment up front.

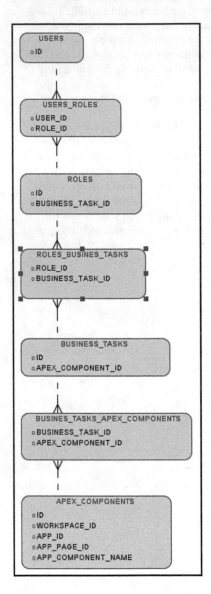

Figure 7-4. *A complete Authorization Entity Relationship Diagram (ERD)*

The USERS and ROLES data can be retrieved from the authentication environment. This is often set up with Oracle Identity and Access Management (IAM), Lightweight Directory Access Protocol (LDAP), or some other external authentication tool. If you don't have access to your external authentication environment, it is a relatively simple task to create your own USERS and ROLES tables; however, you will give yourself an extra task when it comes to keeping the corporate and local lists of users and roles in sync.

Often, individual users are given multiple roles. This many-to-many relationship is achieved by inserting an intersection table, USERS_ROLES, between the USERS and ROLES tables.

The BUSINESS_TASKS table assigns multiple individual business tasks to a role through the ROLES_ BUSINESS_TASKS intersection table. This relationship is highly recommended to make the configuration of authorizations easier for the team that is in charge of authorization maintenance. The business tasks, which are often called privileges or responsibilities, are usually defined in a system's business requirements documentation. The business tasks are defined in terms of what a role can do and what a role cannot do. For example, an Accounts Payable Clerk I might be able to view and approve an invoice payment while an Accounts Payable Clerk II is able to pay the vendor of an approved invoice. This type of structure is common where there is a strict separation of duties required to keep everyone honest and to make sure that there is also the appearance of honesty.

The APEX_COMPONENTS table links the business tasks to the physical software components within the APEX application environment. This relationship is mandatory because it defines which physical APEX components work together to perform the task. Business tasks are generally performed by a user when the user performs a task that was defined in the Business Requirements Document (BRD) by:

- Viewing information that directs the user to an appropriate workflow

- Pressing a button or link that goes to a page or wizard where a task is performed

- Pressing a confirmation button that invokes the process that runs code that performs the task

These points clearly indicate that there are multiple APEX software components, some of which are visible to the end user and some of which are invisible to the end user, that work together to perform a single business task.

It is important to note that a single APEX software component can easily be attached to a number of business tasks. This fact is the genesis of large amounts of unnecessarily complicated code when the authorization environment is poorly designed.

The physical APEX software components are identified by the following columns:

- WORKSPACE_ID

- APP_ID

- APP_PAGE_ID

- APP_COMPONENT_NAME

These columns exactly match the APEX hierarchy of a workspace that contains many applications, applications that contain many pages, and pages that contain many components.

This architecture allows the team to create a versatile authorization environment that supports both coarse and fine-grained strategies. These can be implemented using a single APEX authorization scheme that links a user to an APEX component through the above linkage and its cascading many-to-many relationships. The linkage can be coded as a SQL EXISTS statement on a VIEW that links all of the above tables or as a PL/SQL function that runs multiple lookups against the tables. Test both these strategies to see which performs better in your environment.

Binding APEX Users to Components

Binding the APEX users to physical APEX components is done by populating the tables as suggested.

- The USER table is easy. The data is specific to the individual users. No discussion is required.

- The ROLES table is also relatively easy providing that the Business Requirements Document clearly defines it. If the roles are not clearly defined, you can start with one or two simple roles that will help you get the infrastructure built. Since the architecture is designed to be configurable, you should be able to implement the defined version of the ROLES table as the definition becomes clear.

- The BUSINESS_TASKS table requires a bit more thought by the analyst team. Again, this is relatively easy to populate when the Business Requirements Document defines the tasks well.

Populating the APEX_COMPONENTS data is the tricky bit in this architecture. Two design issues must be addressed:

- *All of the physical APEX components that are involved in performing a business function must be clearly identified.* A simple example would be the ability to create a purchase order; this task, at a minimum, would require the use of a button and a PL/SQL process. This would require two rows in the APEX_COMPONENT table, one for the button and one for the process. This design task requires close cooperation between the analyst, developer, and GUI design teams. In practice, identifying all of the affected components can be quite tricky in a large APEX system that contains many roles and many functions that are intimately related and that potentially involve sensitive data.

- *Find the required value for the APP_COMPONENT_NAME column in the APEX_COMPONENT table.* The value of the APP_COMPONENT_NAME column must be set to the runtime value of the :APP_COMPONENT_NAME substitution string that is populated when the component's authorization scheme is evaluated. The steps for finding this value are discussed next.

Finding the Value of APP_COMPONENT_NAME

The key to finding the value of APP_COMPONENT_NAME for a specific APEX physical component is in the Application Express Views.

Figure 7-5 shows you where to find the link to the Application Express Views in APEX 5.1. The links to the Application Express Views are easily found in earlier versions of APEX in slightly different locations.

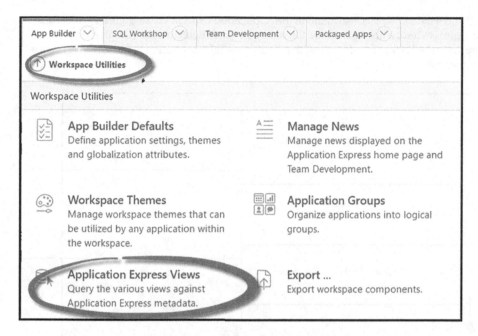

Figure 7-5. *The location of the Application Express Views in APEX 5.1*

In APEX 5.1 there are 149 views that expose all of the APEX metadata that is stored in an entire workspace. To become a proficient APEX developer, you must take the time to explore these views because they contain a treasure trove of data that can potentially help you simplify and automate many programming situations. Authorization is only one tiny aspect of these views.

Now let's look at the steps that are required to find the APP_COMPONENT_NAME for a single physical APEX component; for example, a column in an interactive report. You will be able to find the values for almost all of the other component types using this method. Note that this is not the only method; I am sure many readers can be more creative than I am in this area.

First, look at Listing 7-2. It shows you how an interactive report column, COMMISSION_PERCENT, is created by an application export/import SQL file. The parameter, p_db_column_name, contains the value that is used by the runtime substitution string, :APP_COMPONENT_NAME. In practice, you might need to inspect the application's import/export SQL file in order to be sure that you find the correct column in the Application Express Views by explicitly checking the values. You need to do this only once for each component type. In this case, the APP_COMPONENT_NAME value is found in an Application Express View column name called COLUMN_ALIAS. The mismatch in the names can be confusing, so it is important to check an explicit value so that you are sure that you are looking at the correct column in the view.

Listing 7-2. APEX Import SQL Files Create an Interactive Report Column

```
wwv_flow_api.create_worksheet_column(
 p_id=>wwv_flow_api.id(39252681589330394994)
,p_db_column_name=>'COMMISSION_PERCENT'
,p_display_order=>7
,p_column_identifier=>'G'
,p_column_label=>'Commission Percent'
,p_column_type=>'NUMBER'
,p_static_id=>'COMMISSION_PERCENT'
,p_security_scheme=>wwv_flow_api.id(2674912172155399014)
);
```

The value of `APP_COMPONENT_NAME` is also found in the Application Express Views. Figure 7-6 illustrates a list of Application Express Views whose names are filtered by `IR_` and highlights the view that contains the data in which we are interested. This step shows you that finding useful information in the views can take a bit of time and searching effort.

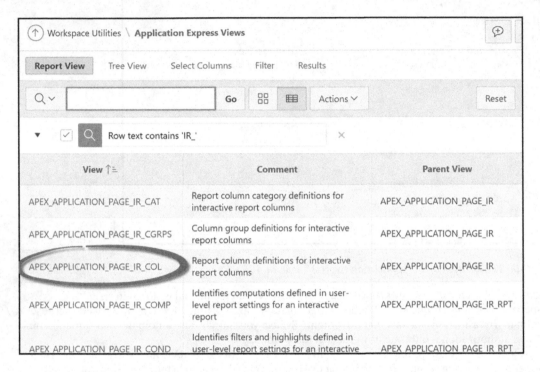

Figure 7-6. *Finding the appropriate Application Express View*

Figure 7-7 highlights the `COLUMN_ALIAS` column that contains the values for the `APP_COMPONENT_NAME`. You can see that the `COMMISSION_PERCENT` row contains the same value as the value illustrated in Listing 7-2.

Report View	Tree View	Select Columns	Filter	**Results**				

Selected View: APEX_APPLICATION_PAGE_IR_COL ⑦   ‹ Filter

WORKSPACE ↑≐	APPLICATION_ID	APPLICATION_NAME	PAGE_ID	REGION_NAME	COLUMN_ALIAS	STATIC_ID	COLUMN_ID
PIAC	53490	APEX by Design	2	Artists	ID	-	39252679158811394990
PIAC	53490	APEX by Design	2	Artists	NAME	-	39252679503973394991
PIAC	53490	APEX by Design	2	Artists	ADDRESS	-	39252679980788394992
PIAC	53490	APEX by Design	2	Artists	COMPANY_NAME	-	39252680342827394992
PIAC	53490	APEX by Design	2	Artists	NEW_COLUMN	-	27387676338191071323
PIAC	53490	APEX by Design	2	Artists	PHONE_NUMBER	-	39252681171764394994
PIAC	53490	APEX by Design	2	Artists	COMMISSION_PERCENT	COMMISSION_PERCENT	39252681589330394994
PIAC	53490	APEX by Design	2	Artists	ACTIVE_YN	-	39252681944076394995
PIAC	53490	APEX by Design	2	Artists	EMAIL_ADDRESS	-	39252680720956394993

Figure 7-7. *APP_COMPONENT_NAME is found in the COLUMN_ALIAS column*

Table 7-1 contains a small sampling of a few APEX views that are used to find the values of APP_COMPONENT_NAME for some of the components that are typically controlled by an authorization scheme. In practice, you will probably need to consider creating your own view, one that groups these views by using UNION statements. The table, while obviously incomplete, shows you the pattern that you are looking for when you inspect the APEX views.

Table 7-1. *Small Sample of APEX Views That Contain the APP_COMPONENT_NAME*

APEX Component	APEX Views That Contain the Value of APP_COMPONENT_NAME	APEX View Column That Contains the Value of APP_COMPONENT_NAME
Interactive Report Region	APEX_APPLICATION_PAGE_REGIONS	REGION_NAME
Interactive Report Column	APEX_APPLICATION_PAGE_IR_COL	COLUMN_ALIAS
Button	APEX_APPLICATION_PAGE_BUTTONS	BUTTON_NAME
Navigation List Entry	APEX_APPLICATION_LIST_ENTRIES	ENTRY_TEXT
PL/SQL Page Process	APEX_APPLICATION_PAGE_PROC	PROCESS_NAME

The main take-away here is that you must explicitly know what value APEX will put into the :APP_COMPONENT_NAME substitution string.

Coding the Authorization Scheme

At runtime, when the authorization schemes are run to determine if a user has permission to see a visible component or to run a procedure, the authorization scheme must determine if a user is connected to the APEX component through the intermediate tables. So what tools or hooks do we have to accomplish the task? Let's step through the authorization process.

First, several runtime parameters must be made available to the authorization scheme. These parameters are readily available in the following substitution strings:

- APP_USER

- WORKSPACE_ID

- APP_ID

- APP_PAGE_ID

- APP_COMPONENT_NAME

The value of APP_USER is available at any time after the user has logged in. The values of WORKSPACE_ID, APP_ID, and APP_PAGE_ID are available after the session has been created. These substitution strings have been a part of APEX from the early days. The value of APP_COMPONENT_NAME is available when an authorization scheme is being evaluated. Two more related substitution strings are also available in the authorization scheme—APP_COMPONENT_ID and APP_COMPONENT_TYPE. The component substitution strings were made available in APEX 5.0. Earlier versions of APEX require a more complex design in order to match the user to a component; we will discuss only APEX 5.x here. Figure 7-8 shows the values of the component substitution strings in debug mode to give you a concrete idea of how they appear in an authorization scheme when it is evaluated.

0.10836	0.00037	Authorization Check: "isTestAuthorization" Caching: "NOCACHE" Component "COLUMN"

0.10873	0.00067	...Execute Statement: declare function x return boolean is begin
		apex_debug.message(':APP_COMPONENT_NAME = ' || :APP_COMPONENT_NAME);
		apex_debug.message(':APP_COMPONENT_TYPE = ' || :APP_COMPONENT_TYPE);
		apex_debug.message(':APP_COMPONENT_ID = ' || :APP_COMPONENT_ID);
		return true ;
		 return null; end; begin wwv_flow.g_boolean := x; end;

0.10940	0.00004	:APP_COMPONENT_NAME = COMMISSION_PERCENT
0.10944	0.00003	:APP_COMPONENT_TYPE = APEX_APPLICATION_PAGE_IR_COL
0.10947	0.00013	:APP_COMPONENT_ID = 39252681589330394994
0.10960	0.00005	......Result = true
0.10964	0.00072	... passed

Figure 7-8. *APP_COMPONENT_ID value displayed in debug mode*

The values of these component substitution strings are used to determine the TRUE or FALSE return value of the authorization scheme. The authorization scheme code can use one of two general patterns:

- Create a view that joins the USER, USERS_ROLES, ROLES, ROLES_BUSINESS_TASKS, BUSINESS_TASKS, BUSINESS_TASKS_APEX_COMPONENTS, and APEX_COMPONENTS tables and then run an EXISTS query to find out if there is a match with the APP_USER and APP_COMPONENT_NAME runtime parameters.

- Run a PL/SQL function that runs several individual lookup queries to determine the value of the authorization scheme.

The choice between the two will depend on your environment. If you are getting the USER and ROLE information from an external source there may be performance issues that will dictate one strategy over the other. Testing in this area is required before making the decision.

In both cases, the authorization's pseudocode might look like this:

- For the component being evaluated, get the value of its `COMPONENT_NAME`.

- Pass the values of `:APP_USER` and `:APP_COMPONENT_NAME` to the authorization scheme.

- Is `APP_COMPONENT_NAME` linked to `APP_USER` through the cascading relationships that link the authorization tables? If so, return true; if not, return false.

Authorization Granularity

Large cloud and enterprise computer systems contain many applications that, in turn, contain possibly hundreds of pages that contain many components. Keeping track of the resulting thousands of individual components that must be secured is a daunting task. Minimizing the complexity of the authorization environment is a key optimization task that will lower cost of development and maintenance, plus lower the risk of security breaches that are due to authorization errors.

We first look at the extreme ends of the authorization granularity continuum and then explore the practical solution that is somewhere in between.

Coarse Grained

At one end of the spectrum, you could build one application for each user role. Authorization would be applied only to the applications. Inside each application, there would be no need to utilize authorization for individual components because the entire application would be tailored explicitly to the role. This strategy might be too extreme for some of you. A more realistic extreme would be to create individual pages in an application for each role.

This strategy would greatly simplify the authorization environment at the cost of a great deal of code duplication. For example, if there are related roles like Accounts Payable I and Accounts Payable II, it is safe to assume that they will probably share many common responsibilities and also have a few minor differences. Building separate applications or pages for these related roles would clearly not be optimal.

Fine Grained

At the other end of the spectrum, you could build a single monolithic application that is made up of pages that support every role. This strategy will remove a great deal of potential code duplication at the cost of building very heavy pages that must support all of the user roles that touch them. Supporting many roles on a single page makes the authorization organization complex; it also can make the User Experience (UX) coding complex when you need to add many Dynamic Actions that tailor the pages to support the individual roles.

Heavy, complex pages are costly to develop, maintain, and document. Maintenance mistakes are easy to make and will make the pages fragile and potentially insecure.

A Mixture of Coarse and Fine Grained Authorization

An optimum strategy lies somewhere between the two extremes of coarse and fine-grained architectures. Finding your "sweet spot" is, as always, the tricky bit.

Finding the authorization sweet spot requires a careful analysis of the business requirements. We first must identify what needs to be done. Second, we need to figure out how the tasks can be done. Finally, we need to figure out who performs the tasks and which mechanical conditions control them. Getting this right requires that we arrange the moving parts in an optimal design.

Areas like administration and configuration functions can take advantage of a cookie application design. For example, an administration application can be designed to maintain the configuration database objects that affect a large system. This administration application could be accessed on a coarse grained basis where only the system administrators are allowed to run the application. In this case, the administration application itself is secured by an authorization scheme and none of the individual components need authorization; this uses the one-role-one-application design.

Business areas are trickier. Related roles like Accounts Payable I and Accounts Payable II will point us to a hybrid design where you might construct a single Accounts Payable application and then accommodate the subtle differences between the related roles through a more granular authorization design.

In an APEX environment, we must search for an optimal trade-off between:

- A simple authorization environment with lots of code duplication

- A complex authorization environment with very little code duplication

I am sure that these design considerations will generate a lot of lively discussion between individual developers, business analysts, trainers, documenters, and folks who will be tasked with maintaining the authorization configuration in the production environment.

Authorization Configuration Pages

The main goal for a well designed authorization environment is to allow changes to be made in production. To achieve this goal, you need to create an application or module that maintains the authorization database objects.

The authorization configuration application can easily be constructed using cascading Tabular Form pages (APEX 5.0 and earlier) or cascading Interactive Grids (APEX 5.1+). In both cases, the general design involves building pages or grids that:

- Maintain the list of users (single sign-on tool or your own custom table)

- Assign one or more roles to a user

- Assign one or more business tasks to a role

- Assign one or more individual APEX components to a business task

Constructing these pages is relatively simple. The most complicated step (and it is really not that complicated) involves building the Lists of Values (LOVs) that support the configuration pages to help the configuration team maintain the configuration environment. The LOVs are easy to construct by using the APEX views. For example, Listing 7-3 shows how you can get a list of components on an APEX page. In your environment, you might choose different columns to display to the configuration team; however, the illustrated code indicates the general approach to mining the APEX views for the metadata that you need for the authorization configuration task.

The actual implementation of the queries will depend on your approach to constructing the authorization configuration application. In practice, you will apply any number of filtering strategies to your design. You would also most probably use an enhanced LOV plug-in to display multiple searchable columns, which would make the configuration team's task much easier.

Listing 7-3. Query That Exposes Components on an APEX Page

```
-- Regions.
select APPLICATION_ID||'-'||PAGE_ID||'-'|| REGION_NAME as COMPONENT_NAME
     , REGION_ID                                 as COMPONENT_ID
from   APEX_APPLICATION_PAGE_REGIONS
where  workspace      = :WORKSPACE
and    APPLICATION_ID = :APP_ID

union all

-- Buttons.
select APPLICATION_ID||'-'||PAGE_ID||'-'||BUTTON_NAME as COMPONENT_NAME
     , BUTTON_ID                                 as COMPONENT_ID
from   APEX_APPLICATION_PAGE_BUTTONS
where  workspace      = :WORKSPACE
and    APPLICATION_ID = :APP_ID

union all

-- Continue with the rest of the component types.
...
```

Component Names

Good names are extremely important in our professional computer programming environment. Good names lead to efficient self-documenting code. Bad names are the source of much wasted time where programmers and configuration personnel need to spend valuable time looking up the meaning of an obtuse or ambiguous component name. Worse, they might get lazy or forgetful and make a guess as to what a component name means; this leads to bugs that are costly to fix.

What are the properties of "good" names? This is an area that generates much controversy. Some programmers insist on keeping component names as short as possible. This makes code entry fast at the expense of maintenance. Other programmers insist on using longer component names that use complete words instead of acronyms and terse names that contain no vowels. This makes code entry a wee bit slower but makes maintenance much easier. The strategy choice, of course, depends on the development team's preference.

The APEX authorization configuration application exposes the APEX component names to a team that is probably not part of the development team. The configuration team will most likely be closer to the business teams. Given this situation, I argue that using longer business friendly names is a trade-off that is worth discussing with both the development and configuration teams. The configuration team will have a much easier time making an environment secure if the APEX component names are meaningful to them and if the names have a clear correlation with the application pages.

Names that will help the configuration team have the following properties:

- They are complete words. Avoid acronyms, terse abbreviations, and "geeky" slang.

- They are business words that correlate with the business requirements.

- They have consistent patterns such as noun-verb or verb-noun.

Oracle 12cR2 now supports table and column name lengths of up to 128 characters. This will help you name things in a more business friendly manner. APEX also allows you to use STATIC_IDs for many of its components. This attribute could be used creatively to help with the authorization configuration work by introducing another way of adding some friendliness to the environment.

Security

Authorization is a security tool; therefore, it is extremely important to organizations that manage sensitive data. There is a strong argument for isolating the authorization configuration application by putting it into its own workspace with a single parsing schema (Figure 7-9). The authorization data is exposed to the consuming schemas by granting only SELECT on the authorization views to the application parsing schemas. Other privileges such as INSERT, UPDATE, and DELETE are not granted. This architecture centralizes all authorization for an entire APEX instance. Other architectures may be considered, but you will find that they will utilize variations on this pattern.

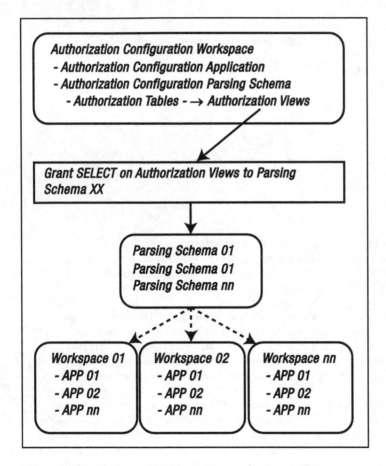

Figure 7-9. Authorization configuration application architecture

Training the Configuration Team

The personnel in the authorization configuration team will probably have business backgrounds as opposed to development backgrounds. They will be intimately familiar with the business requirements; however, they will probably need training in order for them to accurately configure the authorization environment. The main task for them is linking a business requirement to a number of physical APEX components that work together to perform the business tasks. The APEX components can be grouped into two classes—visible and invisible.

The *visible* components are things like navigation links, buttons, report columns, etc. The visible components are relatively easy to configure because the developers can expose visible attributes like link text, labels, and report headers in the authorization configuration drop-down lists.

The *invisible* components are things like PL/SQL processes and application items that have no visible aspect. This is where a good naming convention comes into play. The names must be chosen so that the configuration team can accurately associate the invisible component to a business task. The configuration and development teams should collaborate on the naming conventions for the invisible components. The development team must also inform the configuration team of the importance of adding authorization schemes to the invisible PL/SQL process components and show them how easy it is for a hacker to run the PL/SQL processes on the server if they are not protected by authorization.

Authorization vs. Conditions

Authorizations and conditions can achieve the same result; they control the rendering of a component by returning true or false. I have seen cases where code gets overly complicated and hard to configure and maintain when these two components overlap in their functionality. A good APEX design will clearly use these components for their intended purpose. This is a simple but often abused concept.

Authorization allows a component to render or run when the logged-in user has the explicit permission to use the component.

A condition is used to render or run a component when the correct logical condition exists.

For example, a user with an accounts payable role is allowed to see a button that runs a process that pays an invoice. The authorization scheme, in this case will return true. The condition, on the other hand, will check to see if the status of the invoice is "approved"; if so, the condition function will return true. The bottom line here is that to pay an invoice, both the authorization and condition functions must return true.

Keeping authorization logic separate from conditional logic is an important design principle and a best practice.

Summary

Authorization should be configurable in a production environment; this enables the organization to respond to changes to the permission model without needing to change code that would require testing and a release cycle. APEX contains a built-in access control page that creates an authorization environment declaratively. The built-in access control page can be useful for small, simple application environments but it does not scale. A robust architecture that scales well employs four cascading database entities: users, roles, business tasks, and APEX components. Authorization is controlled at runtime through a special-purpose APEX application that is a simple table maintenance tool that updates these four entities, together with their intersection tables that maintain their many-to-many relationships. A single authorization scheme function is coded to link a user to a physical APEX component through the user, role, business task, and APEX component relationships. A mixture of coarse and fine-grained authorization strategies is designed to achieve an optimum trade-off between keeping the authorization environment as simple as possible and avoiding code redundancy. The authorization design can keep the authorization environment itself secure by isolating it and restricting access to its database objects. The configuration team that manages the authorization environment in production must receive the appropriate training so that they can make changes accurately and securely. Finally, developers must take care to keep authentication and condition logic separate to avoid unnecessary code complexity.

CHAPTER 8

∎ ∎ ∎

GUI Design

Designing a web-based Graphic User Interface (GUI) that pleases absolutely everyone is impossible. That is the bad news. The good news is you can probably please a majority of your users by using APEX, which delivers a good looking and functional GUI at a reasonable cost.

This chapter starts by presenting an overview of GUI design trade-offs and issues. These are strategic topics that must be mulled over by the various teams that are involved in designing the overall product that you are building. The chapter then goes on to discuss the tactical issues that are related to implementing your GUI strategy by using APEX.

To be clear, this chapter is not about creating a graphic design from scratch. That task is best left to professional graphic designers who have studied graphic design and who have spent years practicing that art in the field. Developers are trained to write the code that implements an existing graphic design; in other words, developers receive the output of graphic designers as input. In the APEX context, developers can use one of two GUI design strategies.

- *A graphic design, like the Universal Theme, that is handed to them by the APEX development team.* It is important to note that the APEX development team has exposed many aspects of their graphic design through the Page Designer's declarative interface. If you adjust the default APEX theme styles, I would argue that the resulting GUI should be reviewed by a professional graphic designer to make sure that the colors and other adjustments actually "work" together.

- *A custom graphic design that has been developed by an external graphic designer.* This work requires a developer who is intimately familiar with how APEX has implemented its Theme and Template framework and an expert HTML, CSS, and JavaScript developer. In addition, this work requires a top-notch testing team that has the time and resources to test the application using all of the common web browsers. This testing task never ends because the web browser manufacturers release new versions several times per year and the development team usually has no control over when their end users will upgrade their web browsers. In other words, building a custom theme from scratch in APEX can be a costly option.

In both cases, the developer acts as an assembler of GUI components, not a manufacturer of GUI components. This chapter is about assembling a GUI in an APEX context.

© Patrick Cimolini 2017
P. Cimolini, *Oracle Application Express by Design*, https://doi.org/10.1007/978-1-4842-2427-4_8

GUI Goals

The main purpose of a large cloud or enterprise computer GUI is to allow human beings to keep an abstract logical model of the business in sync with the real business. A key tool for making that happen is a GUI that makes it convenient for human beings to input the appropriate data, easily see and grasp the resulting information, and then quickly take the appropriate action that is indicated by the information. This, of course, is easier said than done.

Now let's look at a few of the considerations that need to be discussed before designing a GUI that will achieve these goals.

The Invisible GUI

First, let's talk about a trap that many GUI developers fall into. To set the stage for this point, please look at Figure 8-1 and think about what you see. Your immediate reaction is probably, "I see a picture of the Mona Lisa". This is a natural reaction because the main focus point in the figure is the artwork.

Figure 8-1. *The invisible frame*

Now ask yourself, "why the frame"? What purpose does it serve? Did you even notice it when you looked at the artwork? Do you care about the frame?

The ornate frame's primary purpose is to draw the viewer's eye to the artwork and to isolate the artwork from the wallpaper behind it. The frame must do its task without calling attention to itself. The craftsperson who assembled the frame is a highly skilled professional who carefully selected an appropriate frame design that suits both the artwork and the background wall. After selection, the craftsperson carefully chose the places to cut the frame wood so that the corners match up smoothly without any glaring mismatches in the frame's pattern. The result of all this hard work is a frame that is, for the artwork viewer, invisible.

Now how does this relate to the trap that I spoke about? Imagine how the frame would be constructed by an immature GUI developer. I suspect that many GUI developers might frame the Mona Lisa with garish high contrast colors, fancy animated flashing lights, and other technical tricks that show off their technical skills; they want to be noticed and they want to impress other GUI developers. Another reason for garish GUIs is driven by sales personnel. They often want to present a product that causes potential buyers to say "oooo and ahhhh" when they first see it. Again, this is a trap because the buyers are seldom tasked with doing the "real" work of the system. The front-line staff can often be irritated over time by an overly garish GUI that subtly impedes getting their work done.

The main take-away here is to guard against building a GUI that calls attention to itself. GUIs must call attention to the work that needs to be done. GUIs must effectively be invisible.

User Experience

The field of User Experience (UX) is huge and it encompasses all of the products in the world. All things that people use come with a UX that is positive, neutral, or negative. My experience with corkscrews is an example. For years I used a cheap corkscrew that was difficult to use. It irritated me every time I opened a bottle of wine because it was hard to use and created awkward moments for me and my dinner guests. One day when I was in my early 60s (I am a slow learner), I saw a fancy corkscrew in a wine store. At that moment it hit me that I could turn a negative UX into a positive UX. With the new corkscrew, I can now easily open a bottle of wine with a bit of a flourish than ends in that delightful pop sound as the cork squeaks out of the bottle. It adds a little bit of fun entertainment for my guests and me. This trivial story clearly illustrates that UX is all about emotion.

Now how does a corkscrew UX relate to a computer UX? Emotion. This is the common factor. The simple act of opening a bottle of wine is, by itself, a rather boring and mundane task; however, it is a small but critical part of a larger social experience that must be done well so that it contributes positively to an evening of food, laughter, and camaraderie. Entering and retrieving computer data is also, by itself, a boring and mundane task. Emotion comes into play when a person is asked to use a computer application to perform a task that affects the business. The positive emotions that come from finishing a "job well done" feel really good. They boost a person's morale and contribute significantly to their mental and physical health. Other side effects include a good performance review, which can lead to a pay raise and promotion. What's not to like about a positive UX?

So how does an APEX programmer go about building an application that makes the end users feel good when they use the application? The high-level answer is twofold:

- *First, the application must be accurate and reliable.* The users must have a high degree of confidence that the information they see is accurate. The application, when asked to perform a task, must do the task reliably and give the users feedback that confirms the result.

- *Second, the application must present information with terms and formats that are clearly understood by the users.* The workflows must be designed so that the users know exactly what actions they need to perform based on the presented information.

These points can be compared to a car. The first point corresponds to a car's engine, which must run smoothly and start reliably. The driver rarely sees the engine and is barely aware that it exists except for the times when it fails. The second point relates to a car's body work, interior comfort, driving "feel," and the appearance of status in society. This is the emotional UX bit.

In light of these two points, how does APEX help developers to build applications with a positive UX?

Point one, accuracy and reliability, comes from the fact that APEX is built on the solid rock of the PL/SQL programming language. PL/SQL has been around for a long time, since Oracle 6 was released in 1988. This language, over time, has been thoroughly debugged and optimized; it works and it works very well indeed. The APEX development environment has provided, since its inception in the early 2000s, an easy-to-use window into the rich world of the Oracle database through its declarative process mechanism. Figure 8-2 illustrates the simplicity of this mechanism. You can declaratively create an APEX process with a type of *PL/SQL Code* and then enter a small bit of PL/SQL that calls PL/SQL packages, your own or Oracle's, in the database. The APEX declarative interface gives you an easy-to-use text editor where you can conveniently enter snippets of PL/SQL that can be validated by clicking the handy check mark. Since APEX resides inside the Oracle database itself, there is no network latency between an APEX application's code and the data it manipulates. This is a good example of the thick database paradigm.

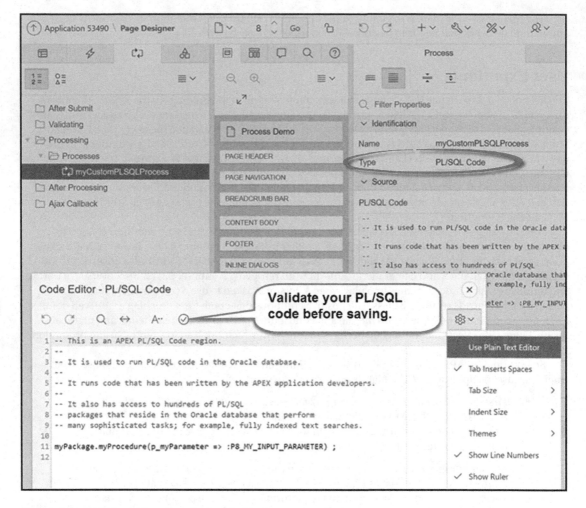

Figure 8-2. *APEX's window into the Oracle database*

Note that it is good practice to move the guts of your PL/SQL into packages. The benefits are:

- *Performance*: Packages are compiled. The PL/SQL snippets in APEX must be parsed and compiled each time they are called.

- *Code reuse*: Handy code in one page can be reused in other pages.

- *Testing/debugging*: Packages can be tested and debugged more efficiently using tools like SQL Developer.

Point two, presentation and workflow, is addressed by APEX's rich and sophisticated presentation mechanism, the Universal Theme for presentation and a rich set of templates for assembling a versatile set of GUI widgets. Figure 8-3 shows you the menu options that are available to you for using the Theme Roller widget to customize the Universal Theme colors and a few visual properties such as button corner rounding. Note that you can add your own CSS, which enables you to append your own CSS classes or override some of the APEX classes. Figure 8-4 illustrates how individual instances of a GUI component's template can be configured declaratively. In this case, an individual region's header can be configured to be visible, hidden, or hidden but accessible. This is an excellent illustration of the "low-code" paradigm in action.

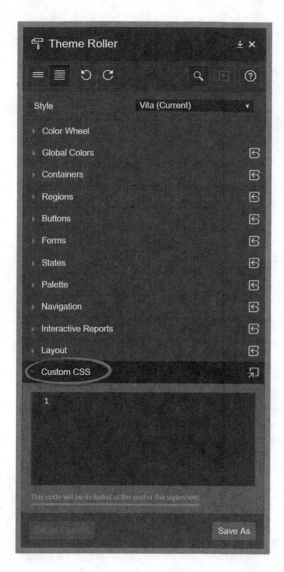

Figure 8-3. Universal Theme declarative configuration via the Theme Roller

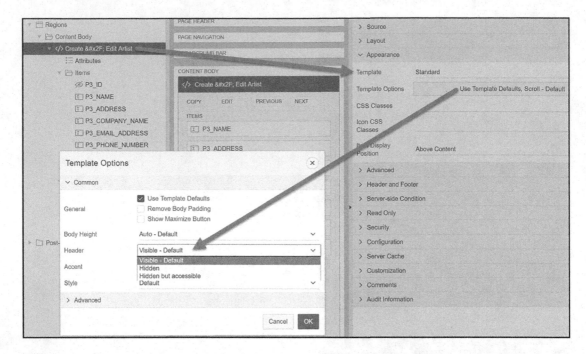

Figure 8-4. Configuring an individual component's template declaratively

APEX's Universal Theme is a wonderful gift. It gives you the ability to build a good looking and responsive user interface that is configurable with no or very little custom code. Remember that you also have the option of building your own APEX theme from scratch. If you do this, you are responsible for writing your own HTML, CSS, and JavaScript and making it work with the APEX substitution strings like #PREVIOUS#, #NEXT#, #BODY#, #SUB_REGIONS#, etc. If you choose to do this, do not underestimate the time and cost that is associated with this strategic design decision.

Your GUI Budget

Okay, so now we have established that a warm, fuzzy UX is a good thing. How much should be spent designing and building it? Before we get too far along with this question, let's do a bit of simple arithmetic to set the stage.

The Cost of a Click

Figure 8-5 is a simple spreadsheet that illustrates how much a single click can cost a company in several contexts. The figure assumes that it costs a company, on average, at total of $100 per hour to employ a person. When 200 employees need to perform a redundant extra click 40 times per day for 200 business days per year, the bottom line cost to the company is approximately $44,444.00 per year. The cost for 2,000 employees balloons to $444,444.00 per year and since one second per click is optimistic, the true cost is probably over a half million per year. These are big numbers.

Sec per click	1		1		1		1
Clicks per Person Per Day	40		40		40		40
Persons	200		500		1000		2000
Business Days per Year	200		200		200		200
sec per hour	3600		3600		3600		3600
$ per hour	$ 100.00	$	100.00	$	100.00	$	100.00
$ per year	**$ 44,444**	**$ 111,111**		**$ 222,222**		**$ 444,444**	

Figure 8-5. *The cost of a click*

Calculations like these should always be kept in mind when designing the GUI for a large computer application. The results are especially interesting to the business owners who fund the projects and expect a profitable Return on Investment (ROI). I suspect that many existing computer applications would have been designed much differently if the business owners were made aware of these numbers.

An extra click is only one example of the many inefficiencies that can be built into a GUI. Other examples include long mouse travel, poorly positioned buttons and links, ambiguous labels, multi-step workflows, inconsistent naming conventions, etc. You might be thinking that you must ruthlessly eliminate all such inefficiency from your GUI design. Be careful, while some of these issues are clearly bad, some are actually desirable design features in some circumstances. For example, multi-step workflows can be inefficient but they can also add clarity to a complex situation. The main design considerations that must be discussed in this context are sloppiness, efficiency, and clarity.

The Sloppy GUI

A sloppy GUI costs more than a neat and tidy GUI. A sloppy GUI is one that is full of ambiguous terms, links, and target titles that do not agree, poor item alignment, geek terminology instead of business terminology, etc. It may have a slightly lower construction cost than a neat and tidy one due to the extra time it takes to lay out the design and think about consistent labels and terminology; however, the sloppy GUI dramatically increases the cost of training, documentation, and maintenance. In addition, a sloppy GUI leads to a lack of trust in the application; if the GUI is sloppy, most users will assume the underlying code is also sloppy. The lack of trust leads to a very negative UX.

Figure 8-6 illustrates a very small number of design principles that contribute to a neat and tidy GUI. Note that adhering to these principles in the context of a low code development environment like APEX is technically easy and relatively efficient. These points are only the tip of the iceberg. Steve Krug's book, *Don't Make Me Think, Revisited,* dives into this topic in more detail. The book is light, entertaining, and a very informative quick read; I highly recommend it.

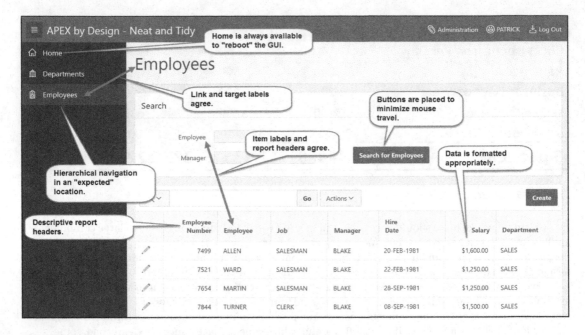

Figure 8-6. *A few design principles in a "neat and tidy" GUI*

Now we will explore a few reasons why sloppy GUIs are built in the first place. Developers do not build sloppy GUIs on purpose. They generally fall into this trap due to lack of guidance and communication.

The guidance can take the form of a rules and guidelines document that articulates the team's standards. This document, which is developed by the team's senior members like the technical leads, could give the developers a checklist for the seemingly trivial cosmetic things that must be done to make a GUI neat and tidy. The time needed to make a GUI neat and tidy is generally fairly trivial once the term "neat and tidy" is explicitly defined for the application's context. Often, important cosmetic tasks do not get done due this lack of design definition.

Communication with other teams is the key for fixing the lack of definition. The business analysts can help in this area by building a glossary of terms early in a project's lifecycle. Doing so will embed a consistent set of words into the application's underlying fabric. For example, if a term is defined before the database is designed, there is a good probability that the database objects like table and column names will be named with the correct terms. Low code development tools like APEX use these database object names as defaults for labels and report headers. Designing a glossary is a good start for making a GUI neat and tidy.

■ **Note**   In multi-team design meetings, everyone must keep in mind that developers have an inside-out perspective while business analysts and end users have an outside-in perspective. For example, when an application feature does not work as expected, developers immediately think of fixing the issue by changing code while the business analysts think of fixing the issue by changing business procedures. Keeping these very different biased perspectives in mind will help teams find optimal solutions that depend on the best benefit to the overall enterprise.

The main take-away here is that taking the time to make a GUI "neat and tidy" adds very little extra cost to the development effort; however, the extra cost will be offset by lower training and documentation costs. This is a key point to be discussed early in the project lifecycle.

Know Your User Community

The term *end user* appears often in design documents. Unfortunately, many design documents assume that the people who will be using the application are a homogenous group. This assumption is wrong. It is dangerous.

Why? Look at Figure 8-7 and think about the trade-off between efficiency and clarity.

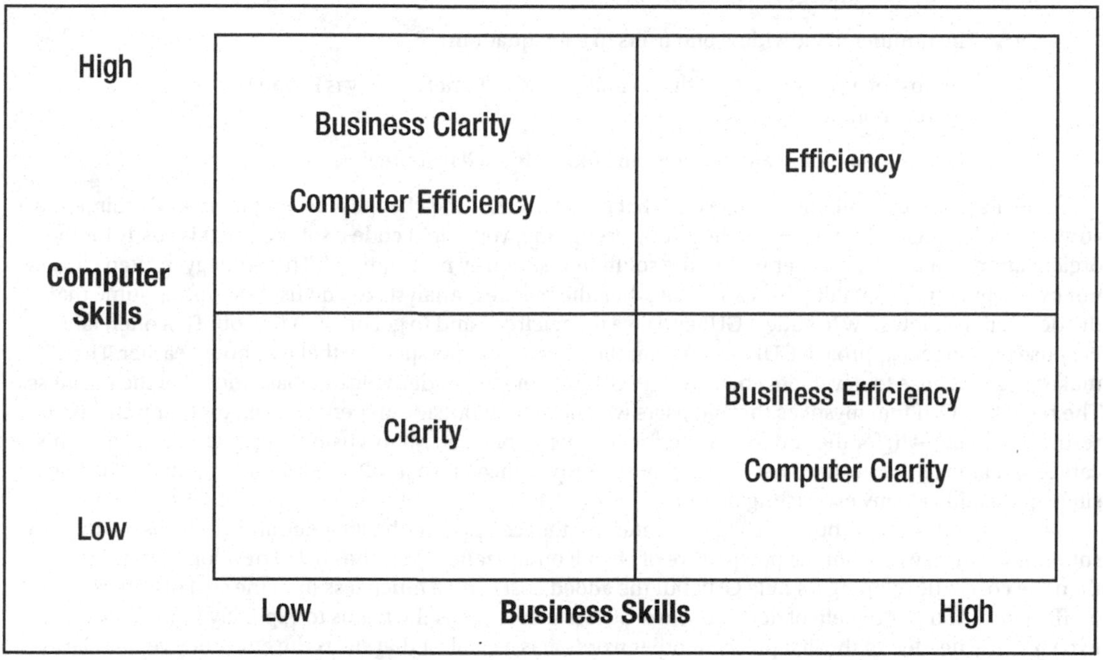

Figure 8-7. *End user GUI needs*

High business skills – high computer skills: These folks are your super users. They generally want to work fast and look for an efficient GUI that enables them to perform both business and computer tasks without a lot of think time and extra clicks. A good example of this type of user is an accountant who is also an expert spreadsheet user who codes Visual Basic Script macros.

High business skills – low computer skills: This quadrant arguably, in many organizations, contains the largest number of end users. These users need an efficient business GUI but also need help when doing "nerdy" tasks such as uploading spreadsheet data into their application. They know their business but do not take on tasks that require programming skills.

Low business skills - high computer skills: These users are the functional opposite of the previous group. They are generally skilled computer users who need help stepping through business workflows. Often, they are senior managers or IT personnel who are called in occasionally to fill in for absent business users. This represents a relatively small number of users.

Low business skills – low computer skills: This user group needs help with both the business and computer functions in an enterprise. They could be new users or users who use the application only occasionally. They need a lot of help in order to complete tasks successfully. For this group, help comes in the form of workflow wizards that hold the users' hands and leads them step-by-step through all of the tasks that are required to complete a task. Generous online help pages and regions are also needed so that key business and computer terms are explicitly defined.

GUI Design for Multiple User Groups

So how do we go about satisfying the diverse needs of these diverse sets of users? There is a spectrum of strategies. First, you could consider building a single GUI; a one-size-fits-all solution. Second, you could consider building a hybrid GUI that caters to both efficiency and clarity. Third, you could consider building a GUI that allows users to configure and personalize their own version of the GUI, one that fits their style of working.

Choosing a design strategy is a function of:

- The number of individual end users in each quadrant.

- The cost of a click, i.e., what the overall cost of GUI inefficiency is in your organization.

- The cost of building and maintaining the various GUI strategies.

The first strategy, building a single GUI that fits all users, is the cheapest development and maintenance strategy. Unfortunately, if you target the wrong user group, you might code a solution that is costly for the organization as a whole; in other words, the solution is seriously non-optimal. This strategy is often chosen, not by design, but by default. This can occur when the business analysts or end users simply assume that the developers know how to code a GUI and give them a free hand to get on with the job. This often fails because developers approach GUI design from their inside-out perspective that was noted earlier. The GUI makes perfect sense to developers because the GUI mirrors the underlying database model of the business. The result is a GUI that mystifies the end users who have their outside-in perspective. Another unfortunate result is that the GUI, for the end user, is neither efficient nor clear. Many custom applications fall into this category; I know this because I have, in my more inexperienced past, built several (okay, many, to be honest) such applications to my everlasting regret.

The second strategy, building a hybrid interface that caters to both efficiency and clarity, is an attractive solution when viewed from the perspective of overall optimization. Yes, the cost of development is higher than the cost of developing a single GUI, but the added cost can be much less than the cost of end user inefficiency. Another benefit of designing two GUIs is that it forces the teams to explicitly think about why two GUIs are needed in the first place. In other words, it is a catalyst that starts the efficiency versus clarity discussion.

The APEX Page Designer is a great example of this hybrid way of thinking. Figure 8-8 shows how an experienced developer creates a new region on a page with one right-click followed by a single click that selects the new region option from a select list. In this case, the region is immediately created with a default name of New; the developer then starts a manual configuration process, which, for an experienced APEX developer, is an efficient way to work.

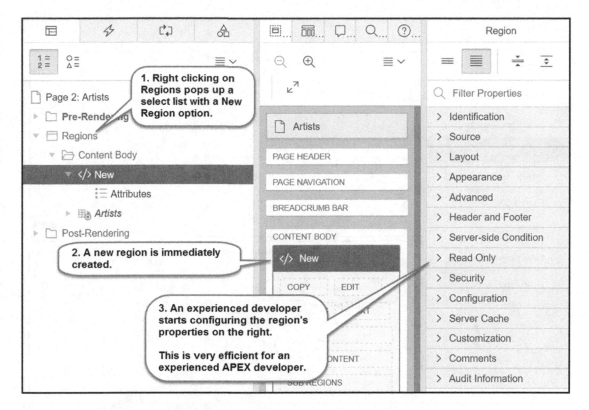

Figure 8-8. Efficiency in creating an APEX region

Figure 8-9, on the other hand, shows how APEX handles the clarity aspect of its GUI. A casual APEX developer can click on the plus sign in the Page Designer, which invokes a wizard that leads the casual user through the important steps of creating a region. This method requires a few more clicks to create a basic region, but the casual developer is asked to set the most important region properties that are required to get a functional region up and running. If this wizard was not available, the casual user who does not know off the top of his or her head which properties are important would probably need to click through many of the property sections to discover, by trial and error, which ones are needed to get a finished basic result.

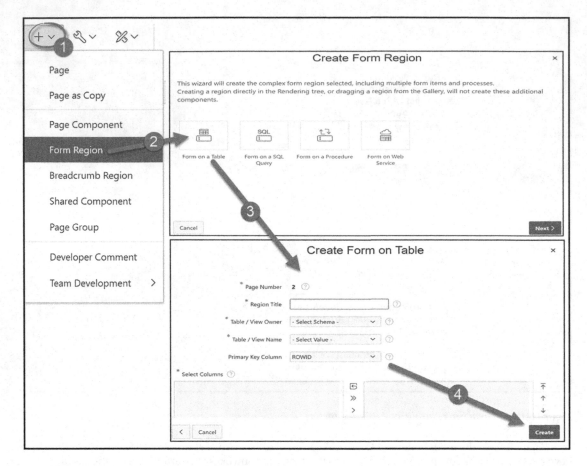

Figure 8-9. *Clarity in creating an APEX region*

The third strategy, adding personalization functions to the GUI, can be considered to be a subset of the first two because personalization functions can be added to either one. Care must be taken when considering this strategy because, if taken too far, it can dramatically increase the cost of:

- Application development and maintenance

- End user training

- Documentation

- Manning the help desk

APEX gives us concrete examples of this strategy in two contexts. The APEX 5.1 Page Designer allows developers to drag and drop its top-most tabs to the left and right. Figure 8-10 illustrates one of the common use cases for this feature, moving the page property editor from its default right-most position to the immediate right of the rendering region. This simple drag-and-drop task saves a significant amount of mouse and eye movement.

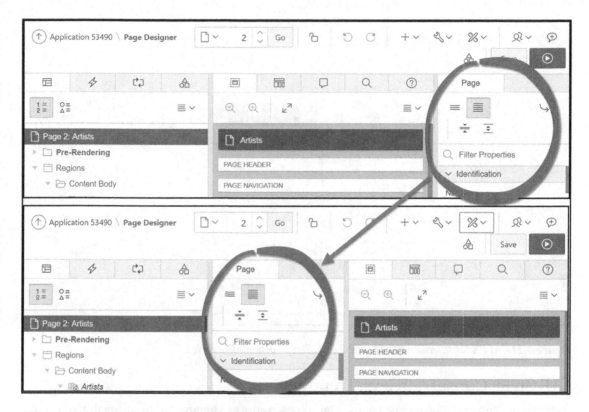

Figure 8-10. *Personalizing the APEX 5.1 Page Designer*

Oracle's APEX development team have also generously included end users in this strategy by adding Interactive Reports long ago in APEX 3.1 (2008) and Interactive Grids in APEX 5.1 (2016). Figure 8-11 shows you the options that are available to end users under an Interactive Grid's Actions menu. This gives end users a tremendous amount of power and flexibility in organizing and visualizing their data. Developers like Interactive Reports and Interactive Grids because they free developers from doing boring and repetitive tasks like reformatting the same report again and again when the end users keep changing their minds about what they want and need; these repetitive task are pushed out to the end users themselves. But this change comes at a cost to the enterprise; the end users must be trained to use these tools and the help desk must be prepared to deal with any end user issues that arise from these powerful tools.

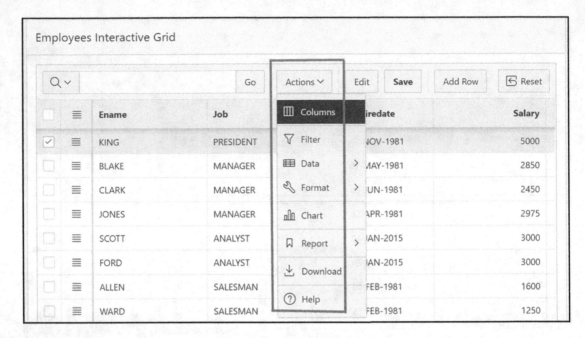

Figure 8-11. *APEX 5.1 Interactive Grids allow end users to personalize their GUI*

GUI Style: Conservative vs. Trendy

An important design decision is whether you want a conservative or a trendy GUI. To answer this, you need to know the tastes of your user community. Figure 8-12 makes the point. We all have a wardrobe of clothing. When we buy a conservative business suit we expect it to last a long time and not go out of style; therefore, we are willing to spend a significant amount of money and look upon the suit as an asset and a good investment that will help us make a living. When we buy trendy party clothes we expect them to be out of fashion very quickly; therefore, we spend very little money on them and treat them as throw-aways.

Figure 8-12. *Conservative vs. trendy illustrated*

The same principle applies to a GUI. Like clothing, GUIs can be conservative or trendy. When I log on to my online banking application I expect to quickly and efficiently check my account balance, pay my bills, and see how my retirement is coming along. In this case, I want an efficient, conservative interface that does not change very often and gives me a strong feeling of security. Banking is boring for me; therefore I want to get in and out of the application quickly and I resent changes that force me to take time to relearn how to perform a task that was previously working well for me. On the other hand, I am also a fan of Formula One car racing. When I log on to the Formula One site, I am looking for entertainment and am open to exploring new features and willing to spend time learning how to use a new widget that enhances the experience of watching races. I expect this GUI to be volatile and actually enjoy the volatility because in this context, it is fun.

The bottom line here is that you must know your audience's needs and wants. Your users need to get their work done. They also need to feel positive about doing the work. There is no correct answer here, just a clear indication that your team needs a serious chat about how to align the GUI to the customers' style.

GUI Layout and Terminology

GUI layout and terminology are closely related to the efficiency versus clarity trade-off.

Highly efficient GUIs that value lots of functionality on a single page tend to favor icons and terse abbreviations as navigation links over more descriptive labels. This tendency recognizes the expensive nature of screen or page real estate. Power users want a lot of functionality packed into a small number of pages.

GUIs that value clarity tend to use longer, more descriptive complete words as navigation links. This, of course, uses more page real estate. In this case, the pages must contain less functionality or force the end users to scroll their pages to find their functionality.

In practice, many GUIs are a blend of the two extremes. Designers must look for the balance that is optimal for their user groups. Probably the best way to discuss some of the principles involved it to work through an example page. Figure 8-13 is an APEX application's home page in the APEX development environment. We will discuss the highlighted points in the figure to give you a very small sampling of some clever GUI design features that create a positive and intuitive UX.

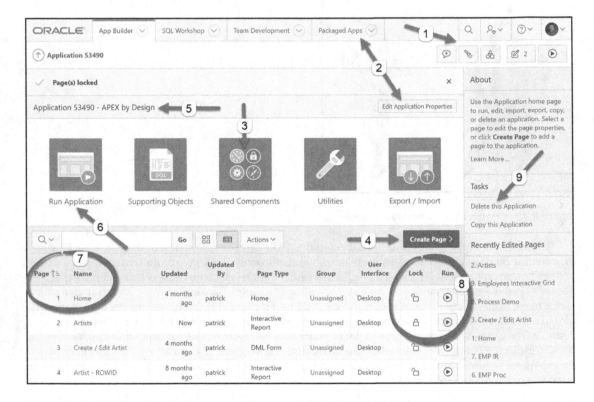

Figure 8-13. *APEX application home page illustrates GUI design principles*

1. Small icons are useful for common and repetitive actions. Since the end users perform these functions often, they learn them very quickly. Tooltips help new users learn the GUI and remind casual users about what the icon represents. The toolbars in the Microsoft the MSOffice applications are another great example of this successful strategy.

2. Abbreviations and acronyms take up less real estate than complete words. If you use abbreviations or acronyms, make sure they are clearly understood by the end users and be consistent with their usage.

3. Previously I have indicated that small, clickable icons are efficient because they consume less page real estate. This set of large icons contradicts this assumption. The large buttons are also efficient for click-through actions where an end user want to bypass a page quickly to get to a child page. This design pattern saves time by allowing the user to quickly click on the large button without needing to take time to find and navigate to a very small icon. This contradiction illustrates an old engineering principle—you must know the rules well enough to know when and how you can safely break them.

4. Hot buttons clearly show the most important actions on a page. They are easy to find and large enough to make clicking on them fast and accurate. Note the right bracket on the button; this illustrates the usage of a common, well understood convention that is used throughout the web world. End users quickly understand that this button leads to another page or wizard.

5. This label in the upper-left area clearly shows the user where he or she is located within the application. Large applications contain many pages, so it is important to give users a sense of place. This is very much like the "you are here" star that you find on maps of shopping malls.

6. The label "Run Application" uses the verb-noun convention to describe the related button's function. The verb tells the user what action is performed by the button and what entity that will be acted upon. Some developers like to use a noun-verb convention which, when entities are listed in documentation, sorts the entities by their names. For example, the noun-verb convention would list all artifacts that are associated with a client object together, while the verb-noun convention would group things by actions like create, update etc. I argue that the verb-noun convention works better for end users because it reads more like a natural sentence. Making end users more efficient is usually more productive for the enterprise than making life marginally easier for developers and technicians.

7. Report headers take up real estate. The terminology should be as terse as possible to save both vertical and horizontal space because the end users usually want to see as many data cells as possible. Here, in this example, note that the Page column header acts as an adjective that describes the Name column header. This is a very subtle UX artifact that adds a significant amount of clarity to the report. Many developers miss this concept when they slap something geeky like "ID" onto a report header.

8. This example highlights the clever use of icons that use a common design pattern. The lock icon is a universally recognized symbol that is easy to represent in an open or locked state. The Run icon employs a right arrowhead that points in the same direction as the right bracket on the Create Page button above. This agreement in shape is another subtle artifact that contributes to a positive UX. These two columns that contain action links are grouped together so they reinforce each other in the user's mind; they are both clearly clickable due to their co-location and verb headings. Okay, the word Lock can be either a noun or a verb but its proximity to the Run column leads one to the verb assumption. I said this stuff was subtle.

9. Delete this Application is a link that is labeled with a complete sentence. The action under this button is important and may have disastrous consequences if it is misused. The word "this" (not to be confused with the JavaScript object of the same name) saves the user from needing to click on the button to see if it will delete another application in the workspace. In other words, it minimizes thinking time for the end user.

The preceding example is by no means a complete introduction into UX design. It is just a cursory illustration of the many points that must be weighed and considered when a team is thinking about how to optimize their GUI layout. For a more extensive and professional treatment of this topic, go to Google's Material Design area at

`https://design.google.com/resources/?gclid=CISchLfA19MCFRSDfgod2nwEiw.`

You should also consider Oracle's Alta UI. It is found at

`http://www.oracle.com/webfolder/ux/middleware/alta/index.html.`

For UI and UX resources, you should Google the terms "oracle application express gui design" and pay special attention to items by Shakeeb Rahman, who leads the APEX UI team at Oracle.

Summary

A GUI is a window into the logical model of a physical business. Users are asked to keep the logical model in sync with the physical model. In addition, they must make business decisions that are based on information that is extracted from the application.

An application's GUI is responsible for making these tasks efficient while at the same time giving the users the feeling of satisfaction that comes with completing a job well done. APEX fulfills this responsibility. APEX provides an extensible GUI framework that is easy on the eyes and extremely functional. It provides a rock-solid window into Oracle's backend database where complex business functions are performed. It provides a GUI framework that gives the user a good looking GUI that can satisfy the need for both efficiency and clarity.

Often, multiple interface styles must be built into a single application. One interface style favors efficiency, another favors clarity. The balance depends on the makeup of the application's user community.

■ ■ ■

Error Handling

"An ounce of prevention is worth a pound of cure." This old saying should be your mantra when handling errors. By far, the best way to handle an error is to prevent it from occurring in the first place.

This chapter discusses proactive measures that can be baked into your APEX architecture that will go a long way in preventing errors from occurring. Aggressive database monitoring shows you how to prevent low-level systems errors from happening. Good Graphical User Interface (GUI) design and defensive coding techniques show you how to keep your end users on the "happy path" as they navigate through their workflow tasks.

The chapter also discusses how to react to errors when they do, in fact, raise their ugly heads. Code instrumentation and the APEX error-handling mechanism play a big role in this discussion.

We will end by reviewing some basic risk-management principles so that you can think about how much cost is appropriate for error mitigation in your environment.

APEX Error Environment

Figure 9-1 shows a high-level overview of the APEX environment with notes about error handling.

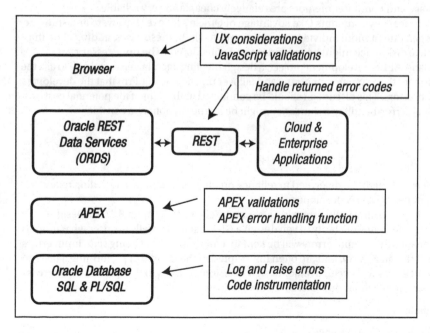

Figure 9-1. *APEX error environment*

© Patrick Cimolini 2017
P. Cimolini, *Oracle Application Express by Design*, https://doi.org/10.1007/978-1-4842-2427-4_9

There are four main areas that must be considered when planning an error-management strategy.

- *First, there is the browser.* This is the only part of an APEX application that an end user sees. JavaScript code can help guide the user to the "happy path" of data entry, which is a great way to prevent errors from happening in the first place. JavaScript validations also can be added here that give the end user immediate feedback that greatly enhances the User Experience (UX).

- *Second, there is the Oracle REST Data Services(ORDS) layer.* This is usually deployed on its own web server. This area is controlled by the enterprise and can take advantage of failover hardware that makes it almost immune to hardware and software system failures. REST is the portal that accesses external cloud and external enterprise applications. The APEX development team and its DBA support group generally have no control over the external environments; therefore, the APEX team must take care to explicitly handle any error codes that might be returned from the external systems.

- *Third, there is the APEX engine.* APEX developers can take advantage of APEX's rich input validation mechanism together with its built-in error-handling capability.

- *Fourth, there is the Oracle database itself that contains many powerful PL/SQL packages plus PL/SQL code that is written by the APEX team.* Here, the primary error-handling tasks involve logging and raising errors when they occur plus code instrumentation that is invaluable to the process of finding and fixing bugs.

System Errors

System errors occur when something in the hardware or operating system environments that support the APEX applications fails for some reason. This can occur when a web server disk becomes full or an Oracle tablespace runs out of room and cannot be extended. System errors are relatively rare in this era, where redundant failover disk storage and computer memory are relatively cheap and very reliable.

Many or most mission-critical environments take advantage of Oracle's failover hardware and software that can run reliably even when one or more individual components crash. In these cases, adding code that tests for system availability like disk space might be redundant and considered to be unnecessary.

Before embarking on a large APEX development project, a design meeting agenda item would be to ask the system engineers and DBAs about their system monitoring and failover practices to confirm that the developers do not need to code for system errors. This discussion should be conducted in the light of the potential cost of a system failure. If the cost is high, error-handling redundancy might be a prudent option to consider.

User Errors

While responding to system errors might be delegated to reliance on failover systems, responding to end user input errors must be handled by APEX developers.

The first line of defense in preventing input errors is a clear and clean GUI. Chapter 8, "GUI Design," talks about designing a GUI for efficiency or clarity. If you design a GUI that clearly tells the user what input is expected, there is a high probability that input errors will be kept to a minimum. That being said, input errors will still occur. End users are busy, in a hurry, and are often interrupted in the middle of performing a task.

Given that end user input errors will occur, a major design decision pertains to the question, "where is the optimal location for a user input validation?" Here we have choices:

- JavaScript validations

- JavaScript validations with AJAX calls

- APEX computations and validations

- Transaction API and constraints

Figure 9-2 illustrates these options. We discuss them in more detail in the following sections.

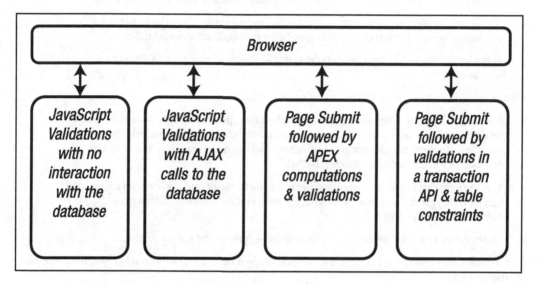

Figure 9-2. *End user input validation strategies*

JavaScript Validations

Validating user inputs exclusively in the browser via JavaScript code (see Figure 9-3) is attractive from a UX perspective.

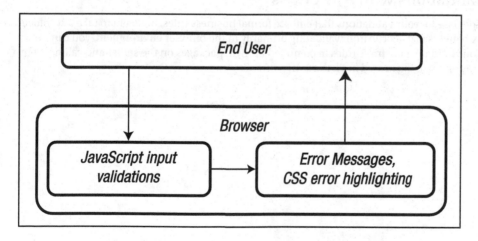

Figure 9-3. *JavaScript validation*

This strategy has the following pros:

- Response is almost instantaneous.

- Error messages have access to labels on the page, which means that the error messages can explicitly reference terminology that is meaningful to the end user.

- No communication with the server is necessary, which minimizes the network traffic and saves the server from doing work that helps the application's scalability.

- Many JavaScript validations can be coded declaratively by using APEX Dynamic Actions.

These attractive features come with the cost of some cons:

- It is easy to hack the browser environment; therefore, pure browser validations must be duplicated on the server to guard against malicious data being entered through the many developer tools that give both developers and hackers easy access to the browser's Document Object Model (DOM).

- Making sure that the logic is identical between the browser and server validations can be tricky given the dramatic language syntax and architecture differences between JavaScript and PL/SQL.

- Maintaining duplicate code bases is an ongoing expense and source of risk.

If you do decide that JavaScript validation is optimal for your environment, strongly consider using the Oracle JET framework.

There is a strong case for writing pure client-side validations for some situations. For example, you can easily block alpha characters from being entered into a numeric field. Data entry validations at the keystroke level can significantly enhance the UX. Another common situation pertains to highlighting errors without affecting a page's layout; this can be accomplished by adding a colored border via a dynamic change to an input's Cascading Style Sheet (CSS) code when the input contains an error.

JavaScript Validations with AJAX Calls

If you want one code base for your validations that enforce formal business rules, but want to take advantage of the attractive UX benefits that accrue from validating primarily in the browser environment, you can consider placing your validation business rules in compiled PL/SQL packages on the server and calling them via an AJAX call. This option is illustrated in Figure 9-4.

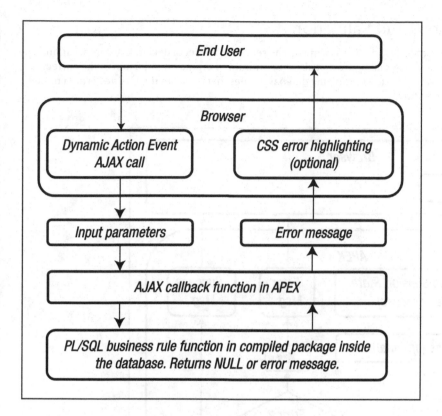

Figure 9-4. *JavaScript Validations with AJAX calls*

This option is like the old saying: "You can't have your cake and eat it, too". The pros are:

- Acceptable UX responsiveness.

- Single PL/SQL container for the formal validation business rules.

- Most JavaScript code can be created via APEX Dynamic Actions.

- The server side code has access to a page's labels via the APEX views.

This option, of course, comes with its own cons.

- The AJAX call must pass data back and forth between the browser and the server. While this is far more efficient than submitting the page and performing a full page refresh, it still can add a bit of time that might be noticeable to the end users as a bit of flicker and momentary hesitation in the GUI.

- The server must do a bit of work, which affects scalability in a small way.

It makes sense to assemble the error message on the server so that the message is consistent no matter where the error is detected. An efficient strategy for coding this type of validation function is to craft it as a function that returns NULL to signify success and returns an error message to signify failure. Page-specific information that helps build user-friendly error messages can be either passed to the server as AJAX parameters or can be looked up from the APEX views.

This strategy is also required when business rule validations need to use sensitive data. Sensitive data must never be sent out to the browser and must always remain securely hidden on the server.

APEX Computations and Validations

When an APEX page is submitted to the APEX engine on the server, a rich set of declarative computations and validations can be employed to make sure that all of the submitted inputs are valid and in the correct format before the data is written into the underlying database tables that make up the business's data model. Figure 9-5 summarizes this feature.

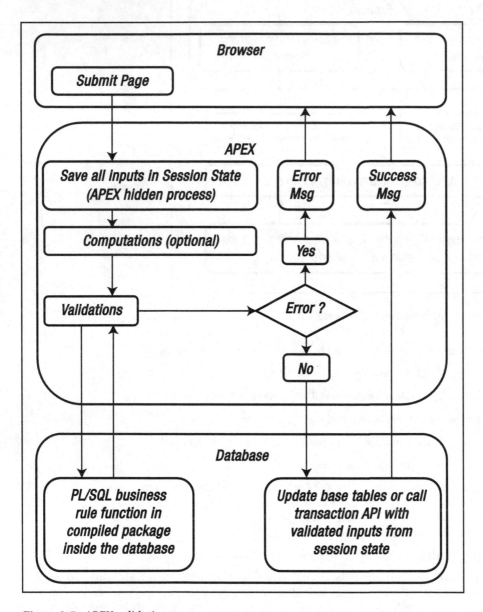

Figure 9-5. *APEX validations*

The end user begins this process by entering data into an APEX page using the browser. When the end user is satisfied with the inputs, an `apex.submit` process in the browser is called, which transmits all of the input values to the APEX engine.

The APEX engine then takes control. The first task copies the input values into their corresponding session state items. This process is invisible to APEX developers so it is always good to remind ourselves that this process exists and what it does; this is one of the key processes that helps us understand how APEX's session state architecture works.

Once all of the inputs from the browser are safely stored in session state, the developer takes over by setting up the computations and validations. Computations are a handy mechanism for reformatting the inputs where necessary. For example, a computation could convert a mixed-case input to uppercase.

An APEX validation is a powerful and versatile mechanism for making sure that a user's input conforms to the enterprise's business rules before being saved in the database. The pros for using the APEX validation mechanism are:

- Code development is fast.

- Maintenance is simple and clear.

- The page validations have access to the page's context so error messages can give the end users page-specific data like #LABEL#, which helps them correct the errors quickly and accurately.

- A validation is usually tied to an individual input item. This enables the error message and format highlighting to explicitly target the offending input.

- Has a rich declarative set of validation types (see Figure 9-6)

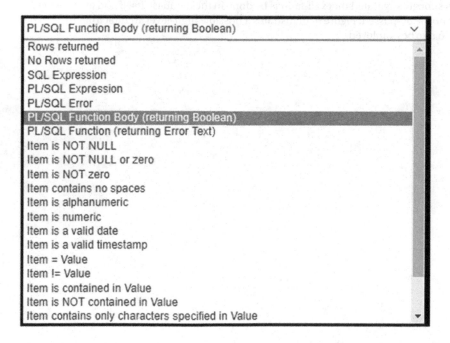

Figure 9-6. *APEX declarative validation options*

There are, of course, some cons to be considered:

- A validation is usually tied to an individual input item (yes, this is listed as a pro as well). Scattering business rules among many individual validations means that the developers do not have a single place where they can see a high-level view of all the business rule validations that are used on a page.

- APEX validations are tied to the APEX application. Many database architects will make strong arguments for using the thick database paradigm (see Chapter 5, "Database Updates"), where all validation business rules are enforced by a secure transaction Application Program Interface (API). This situation can be mitigated by having the APEX validation call a validation function that is stored in the database. Ideally, the validation function would be the same one that is called by the transaction API.

When one or more validations detect an input error, the APEX engine sends error messages back to the browser, where the end user corrects the appropriate inputs. When no errors are found, the APEX engine carries on to update the underlying database tables via direct table updates or via a call to a transaction API. This final step copies the data from APEX's session state, which is temporary storage to the permanent storage in the database tables.

Transaction API and Constraints

We APEX enthusiasts must recognize that APEX is a small cog in the enormous Oracle environment. With this recognition comes the fact that APEX is not the only application that will update a cloud or enterprise database. Therefore, it is strongly suggested that validations be done in the database itself and architected in such a way that they cannot be by-passed. Figure 9-7 illustrates a possible high-level architecture that can be used; other variations can also be employed.

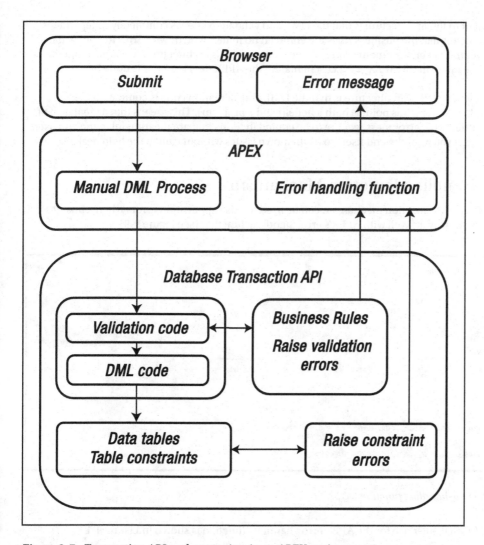

Figure 9-7. *Transaction API and constraints in an APEX environment*

The main observation regarding this scenario is the fact that APEX itself does almost nothing except pass browser inputs directly through to the underlying database without doing any computations or validations. The manual Data Manipulation Language (DML) process contains only one call to one of the transaction API procedures where all of the database transaction processing is done.

Database validations can be enforced by a business rule package that is called by the transaction code API. The validation code checks all of the inputs and records the errors, if any, in an array or a temporary table. The errors are then passed to the APEX error-handling function where they are formatted for presentation to the end user. If no input errors are found, then the DML code fires and updates the database tables. If a table constraint is violated, then an error is raised by the low-level DML process and passed up to the APEX error-handling function just like it is done by the business rule functions. The fundamental rules here are that when one or more errors are detected, the entire transaction is rolled back. If no errors are found, then the transaction is committed to the database and a success message is transmitted to the end user.

The main benefit to this architecture is that the DML and validation code is completely independent from the GUI. This means that the business rules are enforced no matter who or what tries to update data.

The APEX development environment is an explicit example of this architecture. APEX developers never directly update tables in the *APEX_xxxxxx* schema. All the APEX development is done by calling a rich set of APIs.

The main problem with this architecture is that the DML and validation code is completely independent from the GUI (yes, this point is both a benefit and a problem). This means that a great deal of effort must be expended if the error messages are to be crafted in terms that are meaningful to the end user. This is important when you want the end users to fix their own issues without calling the help desk.

APEX Error-Handling Function Mechanism

In all these cases, PL/SQL's exception mechanism can be used to raise application errors when a business rule is violated. This strategy fits well with APEX's error-handling function (see Figure 9-8).

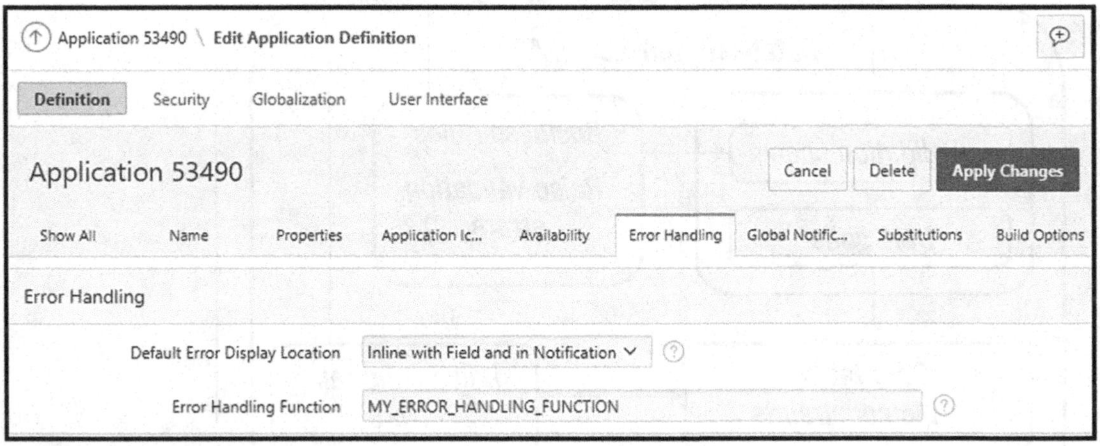

Figure 9-8. *APEX error-handling function*

The required PL/SQL interface for the APEX error-handling function is shown in Listing 9-1.

Listing 9-1. APEX Error-Handling Function

```
function <name of function> (
    p_error in apex_error.t_error )
    return apex_error.t_error_result
```

An APEX error-handling function can be defined in two places within the APEX development tool:

- *Application level*: This is the default location and the error-handling function that is defined here is global to the entire application.

- *Page level*: When an error-handling function is defined on a page, it overrides the application level function. The page level function can be used when you want to provide the end users with error messages that contain information that is aware of the page's context.

PL/SQL code that is embedded inside a database does not know who or what called it; therefore, it throws generic Oracle errors or application errors that developers have coded.

Figure 9-9 illustrates a general outline of a possible architecture for this scenario. Every PL/SQL routine should have an exception block that logs a system or application error in an error log table. After the error has been safely logged, the routine raises the error so that the higher level PL/SQL routines know that a child or grandchild process has returned an error. This strategy of logging and raising errors is independent, at this level, from the APEX environment. The error log table is useful no matter what high-level application or tool calls the PL/SQL code.

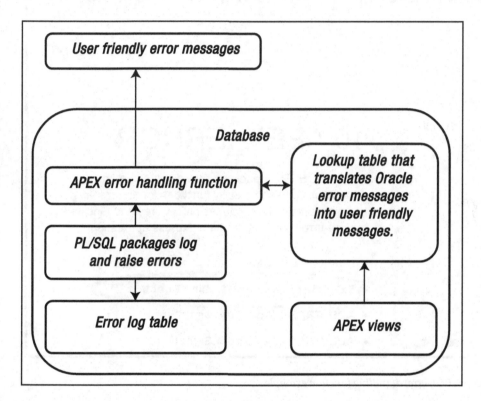

Figure 9-9. APEX error-handling function architecture

In an APEX context, the errors bubble up to the APEX error-handling function, which is the top-most trap for errors. Here, if you choose, you can map low-level generic errors to user friendly error messages by using a lookup table that maps the messages. Since the APEX error-handling function runs within the APEX context, it is aware of substitution strings like APP_ID and APP_PAGE_ID, which can be used to look up meaningful descriptive data from the APEX views. This data can be used to help the end users.

The APEX_ERROR API documentation provides an excellent and explicit example of the error-handling function. This sample code is an excellent springboard that will enable you to quickly tailor it to your specific needs. Figure 9-10 shows you where to find it.

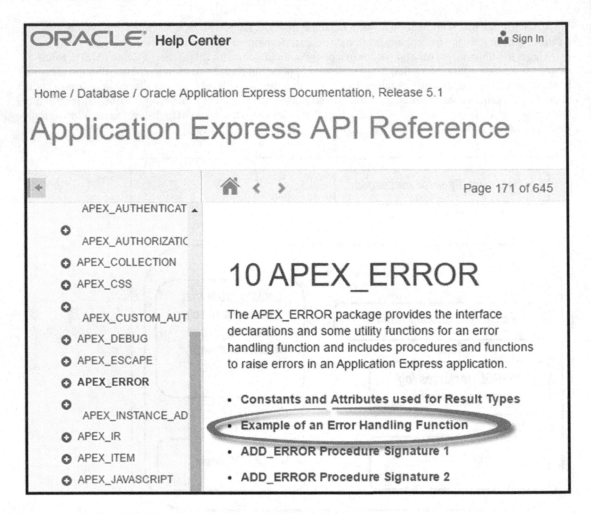

Figure 9-10. *APEX_ERROR error-handling function example*

The Prime Directives of Validation Logic

The prime directives for managing end user validations are:

- *Make it obvious and easy for end users to correct mistakes without resorting to an expensive call to the help desk.* This directive points you to adding validation code directly to the GUI to make it as easy as possible for end users to correct their mistakes.

- *Prevent bad data from being stored in the database.* This directive points you to adding validation code in the database. In effect, you need to build a solid validation wall between the outside world and your data.

The bottom line here is that to satisfy both directives you will most probably need to duplicate your validation code in the GUI, APEX, and database worlds. Designing an optimal error-handling framework will require careful analysis and design where you will pick and choose a hybrid architectural strategy from the suggestions that have been discussed in this section. Note that there are probably other tricks and tips that can be employed in this area; research in this area is very interesting.

Coding Errors

Coding errors should never, ever be promoted to production. This seems like an obvious observation. However, in web-based environments which support complex dynamic logic, coding errors can raise their ugly heads in production.

Syntax Errors

In compiled environments like Oracle's SQL and PL/SQL programming languages, syntax errors are caught automatically for the developers; developers cannot move on until the syntax errors are fixed. This area is not a problem.

However, syntax errors can be a problem in two other areas:

- Browsers
- Dynamic code

Browsers

Browsers are based on an interpreted environment. By design, browsers tolerate sloppy or non-standard HTML and CSS code. This tolerance is largely due to the browser manufacturers' desire to make browsers that are backward compatible with older coding standards and friendly to non-professional programmers. There are probably many more reasons but let's not discuss them here; this is a topic that is best left to a friendly discussion over a coffee or a beer.

It is important to note that HTML and CSS syntax errors affect only the UX and the ability for users to get their work done. These are serious issues that must be addressed; however, the integrity of the underlying database should not be compromised by errors in the browser environment due to the fact that all GUI inputs are untrusted and rigorously validated by server-side code before being committed to the database.

So how do we guard against syntax errors in our browser environment? Here is a checklist that will give you some design topics to think about and discuss among your team:

- *Use APEX's universal theme.* This environment has been rigorously tested by Oracle and gives you a great deal of latitude for declaratively branding your site.

- *Validate your custom HTML and CSS code (if you ignore the first point) by using the validation services that are recommended by the World Wide Web Consortium (W3C) at* https://www.w3.org.

- *Develop coding standards and styles that clearly articulate your team's best practices.* (See Chapter 11, "Rules and Guidelines," for a methodology for documenting standards.)

- *Support only one browser.* This will reduce your GUI coding, testing, and quality assurance costs dramatically. Some end users might grumble about this restriction but the potential cost savings might silence the dissenters.

Dynamic Code

Often, for complex situations, you will find yourselves constructing code dynamically. Dynamic SQL is utilized to satisfy complex reporting requirements. Both dynamic SQL and JavaScript are required when you build your own APEX plug-ins. Dynamic code is rendered at runtime and cannot be pre-checked by a compiler or a code validation tool. Therefore, you must devote extra time for testing and manual code inspections. Special care must be taken to prevent SQL injection and cross-site scripting security issues (see Appendix B for security references).

Logic Errors

Preventing logic errors from being written in your code is a universal problem in all computer programming environments; it is obviously not unique to APEX. The following is a suggested checklist for a development team. Some of the points are unique to APEX.

- *Use APEX's feedback mechanism in your development and test environments.* The feedback mechanism captures the browser type and version together with all of the session state values. Both of these artifacts are valuable when trying to understand and fix an issue or a bug.

- *Run the APEX Advisor often as you develop APEX applications.* The APEX Advisor checks for many APEX specific issues that should be addressed before promoting an application from development to test.

- *Run your APEX applications through a security checker.* Currently, there are two options for you to evaluate—APEXsec and APEX-SERT. These tools are discussed in a bit more detail under the security section in Appendix B.

- *Instrument your code using professional tools like these*:

  - *Logger*: This is a mature open source project that is used to add practical and effective code instrumentation to your PL/SQL environment (`https://github.com/OraOpenSource/Logger`).

  - *Web Tracing Frameworks*: Debug GUI code by using a web tracing framework such as Google's open source project (`https://google.github.io/tracing-framework/index.html`) or the Stack Trace tool (`https://www.stacktracejs.com`). This topic is worth an entire book on its own; these two links are a good starting point for your research in this area.

- *Develop and document a set of practical coding standards for your team.* Emphasize using consistent and defensive coding patterns that you have thoroughly vetted and tested. Document the standards using a practical format like the one suggested in Chapter 11, "Rules and Guidelines". Make sure all of your existing and new personnel know how to find and apply the standards; consider creating an on-boarding course for new hires and get existing developers to review it once a year as a refresher course. Spot check your code to make sure that it complies with your standards.

- *Always use explicit type conversion functions when converting data that is represented by strings into the formal data types.* This is an important point in an APEX context since all data in APEX session state is stored as strings. For example, it is always tempting to pass a session state variable that contains a string representation of a date to a PL/SQL function that expects a formal date parameter without using the TO_DATE function. Explicit type conversion should always be used over implicit type conversion. This point is emphatically backed up by a quote from an article in *Oracle Magazine* (September/October, 2014) by Tom Kyte: "I consider all these implicit conversions to be bugs in the developed code, for the following reasons: ..." The article is titled "On Implicit Conversions and More," and I consider this mandatory reading for anyone who is serious about writing industrial grade software for an Oracle database environment. The article is found at:

```
http://www.oracle.com/technetwork/issue-archive/2014/14-sep/
o54asktom-2279184.html.
```

Risk Management

When you start a design discussion on error prevention and handling, it helps to remind yourself of the basic concepts of risk management.

Two of the fundamental questions in this area concern the amount of money that you are willing to spend to mitigate the effects of errors and what mitigation strategies you need to employ in your environment. Figure 9-11 is a simplistic presentation of the classic probability versus impact quadrants; using this or a related diagram will help your team find an optimal risk-management strategy for your organization.

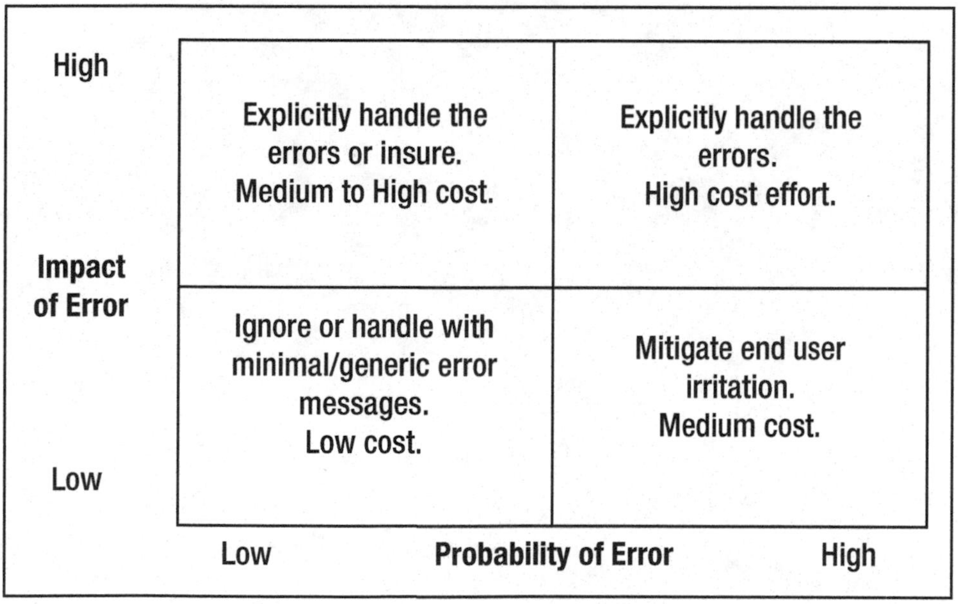

	Probability of Error	
	Low	High
High Impact of Error	Explicitly handle the errors or insure. Medium to High cost.	Explicitly handle the errors. High cost effort.
Low	Ignore or handle with minimal/generic error messages. Low cost.	Mitigate end user irritation. Medium cost.

Figure 9-11. *Risk management—probability versus impact*

Formal risk management is well covered in the Project Management space. I encourage APEX developers to have a chat with your project management team before starting to design your error management strategy. A poorly crafted error management strategy can cost you a lot in terms of budget and schedule overruns during development; maintenance in your production environment can be a nightmare. A well crafted error management strategy, on the other hand, will make the development and maintenance processes efficient, which will in turn increase your team's credibility with the other players in your environment.

Summary

Preventing errors from happening in the first place is the most cost effective error-handling strategy; however, errors will still occur despite your best efforts to prevent them. Error handling in an APEX environment involves selecting an optimum solution that considers making life as easy as possible for the end user while at the same time preventing bad data from entering your database. Making life easy for the end users involves adding client-side validations that give immediate feedback plus providing error messages that enable the end users to fix their own input issues without calling the help desk. Preventing bad data from entering the database involves building a business rule framework that explicitly checks for bad data and blocks it. The business rules can be checked in the GUI's browser environment, in the database via performant AJAX calls, in the APEX processing area, and in the database itself. The last option must be considered mandatory since APEX is not the only data entry tool that will be used in a large cloud or enterprise system. The APEX development environment provides helper utilities that assist developers in keeping their data clean; the utilities include the APEX error-handling function and the APEX Advisor. External tools like Logger can round out the developers' data integrity toolset. Viewing error handling through a risk-management perspective helps the team pick an error mitigation strategy and budget an appropriate amount of cost.

CHAPTER 10

■ ■ ■

Mobile

"Mobile first" is a catch phrase that has been resonating in the software development world for some time now.

But what does "mobile first" really mean and how does it affect the design process in a cloud and enterprise APEX environment? How do we approach the concept of optimal design in a world that is a mix of desktop and mobile devices?

To deal with these questions, we will first explore the types of users who will be impacted by mobile computing devices and their needs and wants in this area. Next we will look at the types of devices that are available together with some of the software that is available to mobile browser applications that need access to device specific hardware. After setting the stage, we can then talk about how APEX fits into the mobile computing space and what APEX specific issues must be explored in order to optimize a design for your environment.

Users First

My opinion is that "users first" comes before "mobile first" when we are designing computer systems. Users are with us forever, whereas technology fads come and go. However, to be fair, mobile technology appears to be more than a mere fad, it appears that the mobile style of interacting with digital data will be with us for a long, long time; most probably, forever. So let's explore how various user groups might utilize mobile technology to get their work done or to enhance their lives in general.

Figure 10-1 illustrates how computer users can be classified within the context of mobile technology. The chapter discusses each group in more detail. Note that this is not an exhaustive list of users, rather it is a starting point that shows you how to start analyzing your users' mobile needs; you will probably have different sub-groups within your individual organizations.

© Patrick Cimolini 2017
P. Cimolini, *Oracle Application Express by Design*, https://doi.org/10.1007/978-1-4842-2427-4_10

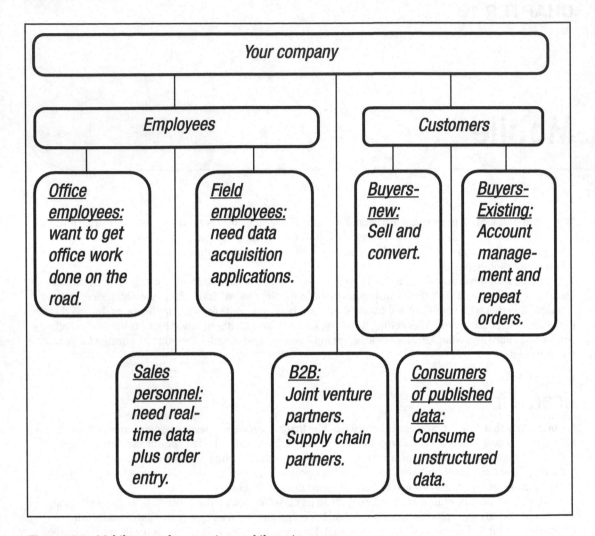

Figure 10-1. *Mobile user sub-groups in a mobile environment*

Internal Company Employees

Your company has employees. Many of your colleagues are office employees who work in a traditional office setting where they work at their own desk, which they rarely leave. Others are field employees whose work regularly takes them outside of the traditional office. There are many examples—sales personnel, emergency workers, police, equipment inspectors, etc. You might think that there is a sharp line that separates these two groups; however, as in most things human, there is a large grey area in between. Let's look at these groups in more detail.

Office Employees

Most office employees work on a desktop computer that is equipped with a large monitor, physical keyboard, and a mouse; standard office kit. So why would they be concerned about using a mobile device to get their daily work done? Here are a few reasons:

- *Time zones*: Your company and its customers may be spread across many time zones, which means that critical issues may arise when your office workers are out of the office.

- *Remote work/flex time*: Companies are allowing office employees to work from home or adjust their office hours to accommodate family schedules, to minimize their commuting time, and to reduce centralized office costs. This means that there will be times when they need to react to an office situation while they are out of the office.

- *Productivity*: Efficient productivity is required in order for companies to survive in a competitive environment. This is a prime driver for staying connected in an efficient manner while out of the office.

A key question to consider when designing mobile applications for office employees is: do they need all of their office functionality on a mobile device or do they only need a subset?

Before answering this question, you must consider some of the following issues:

- *Immediate response time*: Does the issue need to be resolved immediately? If so, can the mobile device provide enough information for the user to accurately respond to the request? When an immediate response is required to a complex request, I would argue that a mobile response is not the correct procedure due the fact that the mobile device might not be able to display enough of the critical information in a format that fully supports the work. Perhaps critical issues should be routed to an available in-office employee who is equipped with the appropriate desktop technology that can display the required data in a format that helps the user deal with the request in a fast, efficient, and accurate manner. This is a business organization design issue rather than a technical design issue. You also must remember that most mobile devices have telephone apps; sometimes a verbal response can be more effective than a digital response when urgent issues arise.

- *Non-urgent response time*: When a response to a complex issue is non-urgent, we might provide the user with a simple interface that allows them to acknowledge the receipt of the issue and a place to enter the estimated time of future resolution; this information would then be logged for future reference. Note that this information could also be transmitted with a simple native text message, e-mail, or phone call; however, the acknowledgement would not be logged within the context of the application. If the mobile user wants to respond to complex issues from their mobile devices, then the application designers will need to decide, in consultation with the mobile users, if they will use a single or multiple responsive desktop pages to fulfill the requirement or develop a separate mobile application to tailor the data entry and UX to the mobile environment. Doing complex work on a mobile device with limited screen real estate is a slow and painful UX experience and should be avoided if possible because accuracy could suffer.

- *Simple issues*: Simple issues that can be handled by an interface that contains small amounts of simple information are ideal candidates for transmitting a responsive desktop page to the mobile device. This is an efficient and cost-effective strategy. The APEX Universal Theme does an excellent job of shrinking desktop pages to fit smaller screen formats and making the mobile data entry process relatively efficient. Unfortunately, the Universal Theme in APEX 5.1 does not support all of the mobile events (like swipe) that mobile users come to expect. In this case, there is argument for developing a separate mobile interface to improve the UX. The APEX development team has indicated that jQuery Mobile will be deprecated in APEX 5.2 and that mobile functionality will be baked into the Universal Theme; this indication has been presented in a blog and at several conference presentations which are all subject to Oracle's "safe harbour" statement which states that comments about future versions are subject to change.

The conversation about moving technology from desktop to mobile environments can be reversed. There are mature mobile technologies that could be moved to the desktop world that might enhance the speed and efficiency of the typical desktop workstation. Here are a few suggestions:

- *Touch screen monitors*: A large desktop touch screen monitor could increase screen navigation efficiency and convenience. To make this work, the physical workspace needs to be designed so that the user can easily and safely interact with the touch screen and still use the regular keyboard and mouse tools.

- *Voice input*: Many people enjoy interacting with their smart phone by using only their voice. Voice recognition software has been around for a long time and its now becoming a relatively mature technology that is still changing very rapidly. If you would like to experiment with this technology in the context of APEX, you will need to investigate software that supports voice recognition through a web browser. Go to your favorite search engine and look up the latest articles that reference the HTML5 Speech Recognition API, browser voice recognition extensions, and the related JavaScript libraries.

Field Employees

Now let's discuss field employees. These folks have legitimate tasks that must be done outside of the office. Mobile computer applications help by:

- Providing real-time information. This is extremely valuable for emergency workers.

- Providing a mechanism for field employees to enter real-time data.

These two points hammer home the important fundamental purpose of digital data entry, which is keeping a company's digital business model in sync with the real world. An up-to-date digital model gives managers and employees the ability to make better decisions which, in turn, provides better service for the company's clients. This is valuable in both the public and private sectors of an economy.

Let's explore a few classes of field employees, discuss their needs, and list some of the design trade-offs that might affect how we build APEX mobile applications to support them.

Let's first talk about sales personnel who are on the road visiting new and existing clients. These road warriors need the two things mentioned in the previous bullet points. The sales personnel also need a mobile interface that helps them to prepare for the sales call and to support them while they are in front of the customer.

The real-time information required to support a sales call includes things like product catalogues, inventory, the status of shipments, notes from previous meetings with the customers, customer profiles, etc. What mobile strategies are available to meet this requirement? Two options come to mind:

- *Big download*: Before a sales call, the sales person could call a large APEX page that contains the likely data that is required during the meeting. The sales person would review the information before the meeting so that questions could be answered without needing to refer to the notes. When the client asks a pointed question that requires a data lookup, the sales person could quickly scroll to the pre-loaded information to get the answer. This strategy could be the only option where mobile connectivity is not available in remote rural settings.

- *Small ad hoc downloads*: Often, sales personnel cannot anticipate a customer's questions. In this case, the sales person might be better served by an interface that serves up small, bite-sized pieces of information that are based on explicit searches. The interface must be fast because the sales person is in front the customer; the flow of conversation and ideas should not be interrupted by waiting for a slow request for critical information. The term "fast" applies to three things: navigation, entry of search criteria, and download time. The interface design must optimize all three input criteria.

Capturing the needs and wants of the customer requires a mobile interface that allows the sales person to capture ad hoc notes that will evolve into a proposal and possibly enter an order. Note that capturing ad hoc notes can be done by using some of the non-APEX hardware features that are built into most mobile devices. For example, mobile devices can record audio or take pictures of a whiteboard; the audio and picture files can be uploaded to the sales person's central computer at a later time. Typing notes into a mobile device is slow and tedious; this should be avoided if possible. If the sales person needs to enter a customer's order in real time, then you will need to decide if the sales person needs the full desktop order entry screen or a version of it that is tailored to mobile devices.

Many mobile and desktop applications can now be controlled by a voice interface. Can you do this with APEX? Yes. A voice-controlled mobile APEX application was demonstrated at the annual Oracle Development Tools User Group (ODTUG) conference, Kscope15. The presenter, Dick Dral, has blogged about this technique and other APEX mobile specific technical issues. Dick's blog is found at:

```
https://dickdral.blogspot.ca
```

■ **Note**   If you are serious about using Oracle Application Express, I highly recommend that you spend a little bit of money on an Oracle Development Tools User Group (ODTUG) membership. Recordings of many Kscope APEX presentations are available at their web site (`http://www.odtug.com`). I also highly recommend attending the Kscope conference, which is usually scheduled for the end of June each year. Kscope has an extremely strong APEX track and you will get to meet many developers on the Oracle APEX development team. Membership is a good value purchase.

Now let's talk about company personnel who visit out of office or away from desk sites to gather data. Examples include folks like public health inspectors, hospital workers, pipeline inspectors, environmental monitors, etc. Here are number of issues that may arise when supporting these use cases:

- *Forms and checklists*: Often, field workers just need to fill in forms and check lists as they inspect a situation in the field. This situation could be satisfied by downloading a responsive APEX desktop page to a tablet.

- *Hands-free interface*: Some situations might require a hands-free interface. An example would be a radio technician who needs both hands while climbing a radio tower. This could require a voice interface.

- *One-handed devices*: You might need to consider building an interface that can be used with one hand, where a touch screen is operated by only the user's thumb. I recently visited a medical device manufacturer that was designing handheld hardware devices that needed to be operated with one hand. This use case does exist.

- *Offline data acquisition*: APEX relies on a live communication link to a central database server. What happens when connectivity is lost? Public health inspectors often find this situation when they descend into deep basements in concrete and steel buildings. Environmental inspectors are often working in areas that have no cell phone coverage. In these cases, the software must automatically detect when connectivity is both lost and regained. When there is no connectivity, data must be stored temporarily on the mobile device and then uploaded and synched with the central database when a reliable connection is re-established. Possible solutions for this issue could be to configure APEX to use the native local storage by using HTML5 technology, installing OracleXE on the mobile device, or looking for a non-APEX solution such as Oracle Application Development Framework (ADF).

■ **Note**   I am an avid APEX fan. The point about offline data acquisition illustrates the need, in a large cloud or enterprise environment, to look outside of the APEX technology stack for optimal solutions. We must never fall into the trap of having a hammer and then seeing every problem as a nail. Most real-world problems need an optimal blend of technologies to meet a company's needs.

This has been a very limited discussion of how APEX can support company personnel when they work away from their office workstations. I hope that this discussion helps you look carefully at your users' true needs with an eye for crafting optimal mobile solutions for them.

Business-to-Business Partners

Often, large companies have business-to-business (B2B) partners. B2B partners can be customers or joint venture partners. These long-term, trusted relationships can be significantly enhanced when the partners expose subsets of their computer processes to each other to enhance efficiency. Examples can be found in many supply chain relationships.

I would argue that external company end users are simply a subset of your internal workforce. These folks need real-time data and access to processes to get their work done.

One of the first questions that must be considered is do you want to expose your internal data and processes to external B2B users through a mobile interface? If so, you must also ask yourselves if you want to allow the external users to access your existing internal system or do you want to build a separate sub-system that exposes only a subset of your functionality. There will be, of course, authentication and authorization issues to be discussed in this area. In the current environment, the 2017 to 2020 timeframe, I suggest that you consider a strategy that takes advantage of the thick database paradigm, where your data and processes are exposed only through a security hardened PL/SQL API. This can be coupled with a RESTful interface to the external world.

Retail Customers

Can APEX be used to service your retail customers? The short answer is yes. The long answer is you need to realize that a retail web site is very different from an internal web site that services your internal employees. Let's explore some of the issues at a high level.

Buyers: New Customers

"Mobile first" has to be considered when you are trying to attract new customers through your web site. A significant segment of your potential market is made up of millennials who were born between 1982 and 2004. If you don't exist on their smart phone, then you do not exist; at least that is what I conclude from observing and listening to my children.

I cannot speak to the art and science of pushing your web site to the top of the Search Engine Optimization (SEO) charts and converting the random web browsing public into cash paying customers because this topic is way out of my field of expertise; however, I can comment on some of the mechanical issues related to designing an APEX public web site.

For a retail web site to be mechanically successful on mobile devices, you must think about the following issues:

- *Speed*: The pages must load quickly. If a page loads slowly, the potential customer knows that your competition is just a few taps away. To achieve this, you must make your pages as light as possible and minimize the number of bytes that must be transferred to the mobile browser. Web server file caching is important to consider. Lazy loading can also help. The trade-off to think about here is the choice between a small number of relatively heavy single pages that contain a lot of functionality versus a large number of very small pages that load quickly. If a page takes time to load, many users will never experience the gorgeous UX that you have crafted because they will not bother to wait for it to load.

- *Interface clarity*: Navigation must be simple and obvious. Never make the customer stop and think. You must handle all of the common touch screen events and respond to them effectively. You must carefully think about the navigation hints, text, or icons; are they clear and obvious to the users? This is a case when you should hire your elderly grandparents to test your site's usability.

- *Readability*: Choose fonts wisely.

- *Shopping cart*: Your shopping cart page must be easy to use and rock solid from a security point of view. A shopping cart page is an exception to the speed point. Navigating to the shopping cart page is not the result of a random search or mild curiosity; therefore, the customer who has already made the decision to buy your product or service will be motivated to wait a bit for the shopping cart page to load; therefore, you can add more code at the expense of more (but not a lot) of load time. For this page you should think about spending a lot of time designing, building, and testing the UX aspect; you may need to evolve through multiple revisions. The customer wants to buy so don't lose them now.

- *Know your market*: Do you need to rebrand your site often? If you are a bank, then probably not. Alternatively, if you are selling skateboards or rhinestone covered cell phone cases to pre-teens, then you will probably need to rebrand often because every year you have a new set of potential customers who will not touch anything that is not branded with the latest transient pop culture fad. In the latter case, you should consider acquiring a team, process, and toolkit that allow you to quickly apply a new graphic design to your APEX mobile application.

Buyers: Existing Customers

Your relationship with a potential customer changes after you convert them into a real customer who you want to repeatedly buy your products and services. Instead of focusing making the first sale to a potential customer, your web site must focus on servicing your existing customer. For example, many online retailers like Amazon provide services like shipment tracking in a convenient manner after you have purchased a product and registered with their site.

Ignore the difference between selling to a potential new customer and servicing an existing customer at your peril. I have a true personal story that illustrates this point. Years ago I signed up with a mobile phone network provider and was happy with the mechanical service that they provided; my phone worked, I could read my e-mails on my phone, and I could easily send texts to my wife. I live in Canada and my professional consulting work often takes me to other countries; therefore, I needed to buy temporary roaming packages. My provider offered this service but finding it on their web site was very difficult because the link was buried in a slow loading and very noisy page that was shouting and yelling at me about the company's new phones and products. The link was there but it took time to find it because it was buried in an obscure location in small muted text. Also, several times I bought the roaming package and did not receive a confirmation so I had to phone their human support line to make sure the roaming package was in effect. UX is primarily about emotion and this site made me angry, it wasted my time, and it increased my stress level. Recently, I finally took the time to research another provider who "gets it"; their site has a sales component but it also provides a fast and intuitive interface that allows existing customers to manage their account and to quickly and reliably buy temporary add-ons like roaming.

How does this story affect your mobile APEX design? You might consider building separate mobile applications or at least separate modules within a single application that are tailored to customer context. The take-away here is that when you are designing a public web site that serves your retail customers, do a good job of building:

- A sales site that concentrates on converting prospective customers into cash paying real customers.

- An account management site that makes it easy for existing customers to manage their existing account so that they come back and become loyal repeat clients.

Mobile applications often need to ask users for their credit card numbers. Handling sensitive information is not unique to APEX and can be handled effectively using Oracle's rich set of security tools. One security aspect of APEX that is worth mentioning here is Session State Encryption. Figure 10-2 shows you where this is set up for each individual input item and Figure 10-3 shows how the encrypted data is actually stored in session state. Note that this feature encrypts only APEX's session state. You must also enable encryption for this field in the database itself so that the sensitive data is encrypted in both the database and in the many hidden tables and log files that Oracle uses to support its entire functionality.

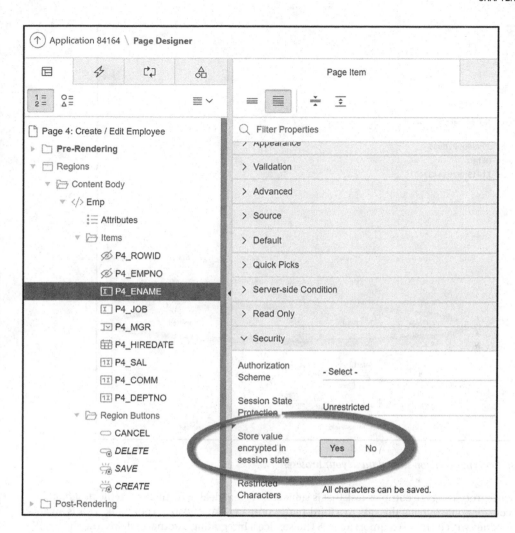

Figure 10-2. *Setting up session state encryption*

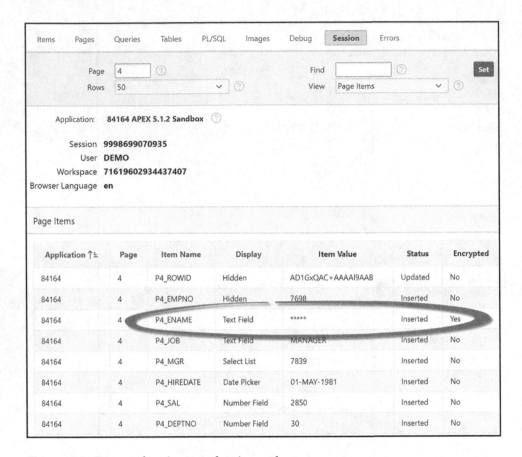

Figure 10-3. *Encrypted session state data in your browser*

Credit card processing is a complex task that is subject to a great deal of regulation. At the design phase, you should consider out sourcing this task to a third-party company like PayPal or your bank. This is an area where APEX shines with its robust support for RESTful services. Integrating external systems into the APEX framework is relatively easy task, providing that the external system provides a documented API. Most large businesses and service providers expose their business functions through robust APIs.

Publishing Public Data

Many public and corporate entities must publish large amounts of unstructured data. Governments, at all levels, need to publish laws, regulations, and responses to freedom of information requests. News sites also publish this type of data. The public has grown to expect this type of information to be available on their mobile devices.

Can APEX be used to publish large amounts of unstructured data from a mobile application? The short answer is yes; but is it the best tool available? For this use case, I recommend that you do a bit of research in the area of content management solutions. Start by looking Oracle WebCenter Content, which provides much more functionality than just rendering data on a mobile device. Managing a document through its full lifecycle is a complex task that mature content management systems already support.

This design point is a great illustration of the principle, "don't reinvent the wheel". APEX could be used to create a content management system, but why do it if existing products already provide the service and can be integrated with your APEX framework? Now if your content management needs are simple, you will need to have the "buy versus build" conversation with your team. If you only need a subset of content management functionality, then APEX could easily be on your short list of tools.

Device Choices

I don't know about you, but I get dizzy when I look at all of the options regarding mobile devices. The number of choices is overwhelming and new products are continually coming into the market. To make things worse, the definition of laptops, tablets, and smart phones has become blurred as their physical sizes change and the computing power increases. Let's see how APEX fits into this fuzzy world of mobile software and hardware.

APEX is a server-based technology that needs only a modern web browser that conforms to the World Wide Web Consortium (W3C) standards on the mobile device. A reliable connection between the server and the client is also required. Happily, both of these requirements are now met by most mobile devices and mobile network providers.

Let's now look at some of the mobile device configurations that can affect the design of your APEX web pages.

- *Corporate versus personal devices*: Some companies provide corporate mobile devices to their mobile employees. This environment makes your design task much easier because you need to support only a small number of devices with explicitly known characteristics. This is a great benefit in cases where your mobile application must interact with the mobile device's hardware like the camera and Global Positioning System (GPS) coordinates. If you must support the employees' personal devices, then you will need to do a bit more work. For example, you will need to detect the type of operating system that is on the mobile device so that you can download the appropriate JavaScript libraries when you need to interact with the hardware.

- *Large versus small screen size*: Screen size can have a profound effect on your mobile page design. If your users are using larger screens, then you would consider building your APEX application with the responsive Universal Theme (UT). The UT does an excellent job of supporting varying screen sizes. If your users are using small screens, then you might need to consider using APEX's mobile user interface. This interface takes advantage of the jQuery mobile library, which supports touch screen events that can improve the user experience (UX). Note that APEX 5.2 might depricate jQuery Mobile and move its functionality into the Universal Theme; we await APEX 5.2 with great anticipation.

- *Physical versus on-screen keyboard*: Some tablets come equipped with a detachable keyboard. This feature helps to support applications that require a significant amount of data entry. Using a detachable keyboard eliminates the need for an on-screen touch keyboard. Touch keyboards obscure data; this might be an issue for users who need to see a large amount of data on the screen to support their data entry choices.

Native vs. Browser/Server

Designing a large cloud and enterprise software system is usually done with a number of stakeholders. The topic of native versus browser/server architectures will most probably arise. We cannot assume that everyone will be initially on board with choosing APEX as the optimal mobile technology. There will be strong opinions on both sides of the fence, so we will discuss a few of the key points to help the decision process.

Native Applications

Native applications have significant pros. Some of them are:

- *Performance*: The native mobile application is downloaded one time and is stored on the user's device itself. Therefore, when the application runs, only data is transferred over the wireless connection. This feature makes the native application fast.

- *Hardware access*: The native applications are written using a language that is supported by the device's built-in operation system (OS). Programmers then have direct access to the device's hardware and other software tools like GPS, camera, local storage, and contact lists, etc. This greatly enhances the UX.

- *Offline operation*: When a user loses the wireless connection, the native application can still operate by using local storage. The local data can then be sent to the server at a later time when the connection is restored.

There are, of course a few downsides to using native applications. Here are a few:

- *Multiple programming languages*: You need to write separate native applications for each device that you need to support. Apple and Android devices use different operating systems, which, in turn, need different application programming languages. The choices that are available can include languages like Java, C++, Objective C, C#, etc. This space is constantly changing with new versions of existing languages coming out together with entirely new languages and frameworks. The optimum language choice is far beyond the scope of this book; it is one of those decisions that is prefixed with "it depends". If you are an Oracle shop, you might seriously consider outsourcing this development and testing effort.

- *Version support*: Each end user is responsible for downloading and installing your software on their mobile devices. This can cause problems when you release new revisions of your software. Your server must be able to support multiple mobile software versions or you must make your software aware of the latest version so that it can prompt the user to download the latest version.

- *App store*: Native mobile applications need to be downloaded by individual users. You need to register you application with an application store, commonly referred to as an "app store". Your applications must adhere to the standards that are required by each app store.

Browser/Server Applications

APEX uses a simple browser/server architecture. This is true for both desktop and mobile applications. One hundred percent of an APEX application resides primarily in an Oracle database and secondarily on a web server. Zero percent of the application resides on the client device. Here are some of the advantages of this architecture:

- *Single programming language*: APEX uses only the browser on all of its client desktop and mobile devices. Therefore, a single code base supports all flavors of mobile devices, which dramatically reduces the cost of mobile development and testing.

- *Version support*: Your application resides on a central server. Nothing is stored on the mobile device. This makes new versions of your application instantly available to all mobile users as soon as the production server is updated. This is no need to use an app store. You do not need to be concerned with end users running an out-of-date version of the application.

To be fair and realistic, we must also discuss some of the downsides of this architecture:

- *Performance*: APEX must transfer both the application code and data to the mobile device. This, of course, takes time when the transfer is done over a wireless mobile network. This issue is becoming less of a problem because wireless mobile network technologies are getting faster and faster over time. Also, once an APEX page is loaded into a mobile browser, it can take advantage of AJAX technology that transmits only small packets of data. AJAX can dramatically enhance the UX.

- *Hardware access*: In the past, browsers did not natively support direct access to a mobile device's hardware. This situation is changing with new HTML5 features coming online. Also, there are many JavaScript libraries—Apache Cordova (formerly PhoneGap) for example—that are available to give APEX access to a mobile device's hardware and OS environments. These libraries are tailored to the mobile device's hardware and OS. Therefore, your APEX application should be able to detect the mobile environment and only download the JavaScript library that works on the specific device. You must never download a library that a device cannot use; this will affect performance negatively.

- *Offline operation*: The inability to operate when a mobile device loses its wireless connection is a major downside of server-based mobile architectures. Often, it can be a classic "show stopper" that can disqualify a tool like APEX from being considered as a mobile option. Currently, there is no best practice available for this situation. I can, however, make a few suggestions. If you have a mobile tablet with sufficient capacity, you could consider installing OracleXE on the tablet and use it when connectivity is lost. You can also explore two coding options that have relatively recently been devised. The first is a slide deck titled "APEX Unplugged" by Dan McGhan. It can be found at `http://bit.ly/2vexE8M`. I had the pleasure seeing Dan present this topic at Oracle Open World and found the approach intriguing, albeit a bit code-heavy.

Hybrid Mobile Applications

Is there a middle ground between native and browser/server mobile applications? Yes. If you want to stay with the Oracle technology stack and take advantage of a low code development environment, you should look at Oracle Mobile Application Framework (MAF).

There is a very good blog post titled, "Want to Bring Your APEX Application to iOS and Android? You should consider the Oracle Mobile Application Framework!" by Frédéric Desbiens. It can be found at `http://bit.ly/2wuaNua`. This discusses MAF with an APEX perspective in mind.

APEX in a Mobile World

Okay, if you have, after due consideration of other technologies, decided to build mobile APEX applications, what APEX specific design decisions must be made? Let's have a look while remembering the "users first" discussion.

■ **Note** There is a book, called *Oracle Application Express for Mobile Web Applications*, by Roel Hartman, Christian Rokitta, and David Peake (Apress, 2013). This book was written for APEX 4.2, but it contains many insights that are still relevant for APEX 5.x. If you are going to develop a mobile APEX application, I suggest that you read this book.

Responsive vs. jQuery Mobile

Choosing the underlying user interface is a high impact decision. You can build a single application using the Universal Theme (UT) and let its responsive technology adapt the desktop pages to any size mobile display. Alternatively, you can build a mobile application using APEX's mobile theme that utilizes the jQuery Mobile framework.

I would argue that for a large APEX system that contains multiple modules and many distinct use cases, you will probably employ both user interfaces. To deploy this strategy, you would probably break your APEX environments into many discrete APEX cookie applications. These cookie applications can be a mixture of desktop and mobile interfaces. This strategy requires a certain amount of training and explanation. Most users today have personal smart phones, so I would argue that the training component would not be too onerous.

Selecting the appropriate user interface will probably involve building a few proof-of-concept applications. These would help users select the interface that most closely meets their needs. APEX 5.2 may completely eliminate the need for choosing between Responsive versus jQuery Mobile since it might depricate jQuery Mobile and add significant mobile functionality to the Universal Theme; we await APEX 5.2 with a great deal of anticipation.

One vs. Two APEX Apps

Another APEX specific decision to make is related to building one application that contains both a desktop and a mobile version of the application versus building two separate applications, one for desktop and one for mobile.

APEX does a good job of allowing you to merge desktop and mobile functionality into one physical application. APEX can detect, at logon time, what kind of device is requesting a page and then serve up the appropriate pages, desktop or mobile, for that session. This is very convenient.

In most of this book, I merely present choices that need to be discussed in light of your particular environment. In this area, however, I believe creating separate applications for desktop and mobile interfaces is the best option. The reasons are:

- *Session management*: There are two important security parameters that should be set differently for desktop and mobile situations. These are "Maximum Session Length" and "Maximum Session Idle Time". Figure 10-4 shows you where these parameters are set for an individually application; default values can also be set at the APEX instance and workspace levels. In a desktop environment that's usually located inside a secure office setting, these values are usually set to relatively high values to avoid irritating end users by forcing them to continually re-log in. On the other hand, in a mobile environment that's located in unsecure public places, these values are usually set to very small values to recognize the very real risk of theft. Currently, in APEX 5.1.2, these two parameters are applied to both the desktop and mobile interfaces. This situation by itself is a strong argument for separate applications.

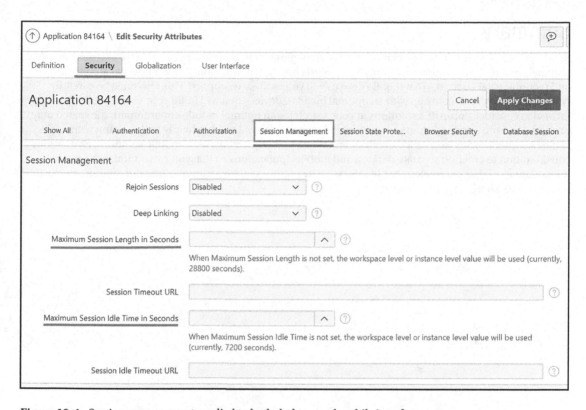

Figure 10-4. Session management applied to both desktop and mobile interfaces

- *Security*: Some transactions are important and have significant impact on the organization, for example, invoice approvals. If these types of transactions are exposed in a mobile setting, there is argument for asking the user to authenticate before being allowed to perform the action. This is very tedious when the user must type their password repeatedly on an awkward, small touch keyboard. This could be mitigated by allowing the user to authenticate using biometrics such as a fingerprint or iris scan through the device's camera. In this case, APEX would need to be set up to interact with the hardware and OS.

- *Release management*: The ongoing evolution of both the desktop and mobile environments usually entails multiple release cycles. Given that the desktop and mobile applications often serve very different use cases, you will find that building a single application would add complication to the source code management and release cycle efforts. If both interfaces are in one application, a release to production will obviously include both interfaces. This is awkward to control if one interface must be released before the other is ready to go. This will cause more branching and merging in the source code area and make an already messy task doubly messy.

Summary

Before you can begin to look at technical mobile strategies you must first consider your user community and their needs. A very careful and complete analysis here will enable you to make optimal architectural and technological choices. What mobile devices will your software support? This also must be carefully considered in order to come up with an optimal blend of devices that will fulfill your users' needs. You must also consider non-APEX solutions in your search for an optimal mobile environment; the search may prevent you from reinventing one or more wheels because there are some handy mobile frameworks that can be integrated with your APEX environment. When you implement APEX mobile solutions, give serious consideration to creating separate desktop and mobile applications so that you can optimize the session management timing parameters, harden the security around sensitive transactions, and minimize release cycle complication.

■ ■ ■

Rules and Guidelines

So your team is well on its way to coming together. You have gone through the team formation steps of:

- *Forming—check*: You have met and shaken hands.

- *Storming—check*: You had discussions, some heated, about how to best use APEX in your environment.

- *Norming—work in progress*: You are now selecting the optimal set of compromises and strategies that you will use to go forward in the next step of Performing.

- *Performing—to do.*

The million dollar question is how do you go about Norming?

I, and some of my teams, have achieved good results by creating a standards document that is based on a rules and guidelines format. Rules and guidelines describe, in a seriously practical manner, how your team will use APEX in the optimal manner that you have tailored to your specific environment.

■ **Note** A rules and guidelines document is not unique to APEX. The tool is universal and can be used by teams in many diverse situations. I was introduced to the concept in the late 1990s by a mentor, Jack Stephenson, who was in charge of a large project that involved a Visual Basic 6 application that worked with an Oracle database. When I joined the team, Jack gave me the team's rules and guidelines document. Reading it brought me up to speed very quickly.

Recently, I have had the pleasure of working with my friend and colleague, Martin D'Souza, who added new ideas to this topic that have dramatically improved the execution of the concept.

Why Standards?

Why does a large team need a standards document? A few good reasons follow.

Consistency

The primary benefit of standards is consistency. Consistency in this context means that a coding task that is repeated many times is done in the same manner throughout the application. This is often referred to as an application's plumbing. Consistent plumbing allows developers to work on many modules within a large application without having to learn three or four plumbing styles; rather, the developers focus immediately on the business rules instead of wasting time on learning cosmetic differences that add little or no value.

Figure 11-1 illustrates this concept where two developers develop two modules and then switch modules for maintenance. This strategy allows both developers to understand the business rules for both modules. Sharing the business knowledge is important for succession planning and accounting for times when individual developers are temporarily unavailable.

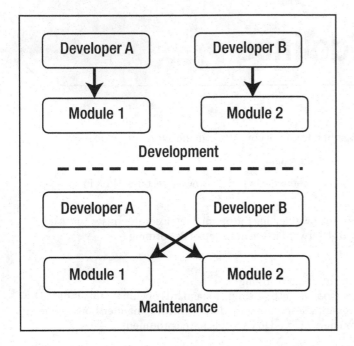

Figure 11-1. *Consistency allows developers to easily move to new modules*

Standardize Low Value Decisions

In most software development environments there are many low value decisions that developers must make daily. Often, if there is no guidance, developers can waste time dithering over making one of these low value decisions. When a standards document makes the decision for the developer, no time is wasted; the developer picks the appropriate option immediately. This also supports the principle of consistency.

For example, Figure 11-2 shows the long list of APEX validations. Standardizing on one option, say PL/SQL Function Body (returning Boolean), will eliminate the dithering time and give every validation in the application the same structure and format. You could also standardize on a small sub-set of validations; this strategy is a compromise between eliminating dithering time and taking advantage of APEX's declarative environment, which also saves time.

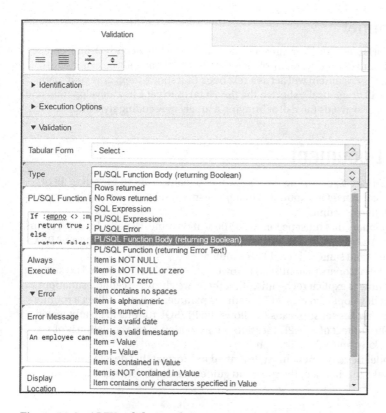

Figure 11-2. APEX validation choices

Repository for New Ideas

A rules and guidelines format is ideally suited for evaluating new ideas that will enhance your standards. As a development team constructs a large application, they will learn a lot of new things and will find better and more efficient ways of doing things. New technologies will also come into play. Team members can add new ideas to the standards as suggestions so that the team, as a whole, can evaluate and comment on them. New ideas can then be adopted, rejected, or deferred to a future time. This strategy explicitly acknowledges the inherent plasticity of the art of software development.

Manage Stakeholder Expectations

A well written and organized standards document is an excellent negotiating tool; it can go a long way in convincing external stakeholders that the development team knows what it is doing and that the development team's standards will, in fact, produce a result that is optimized for the entire organization. Too often, external teams request features that fulfill a single need from a very narrow perspective. Filling such narrow needs can often de-optimize an application and compromise the goals and needs of other, important stakeholders. A standards document is like a steering wheel; it keeps you pointed in the correct long-term direction and keeps you on a paved highway rather that following a meandering dirt track.

On-Boarding New Personnel

There is always personnel turnover in a large team. New hires need an explicit technical on-boarding course if they are to come up to speed quickly and efficiently. Many of the new hires might already be experienced APEX developers; however, the standards document will act as a text book that shows them how your team uses APEX. The standards document will dramatically shorten the time it takes to get a new developer up and running with the team's coding style. It also avoids the risk of bringing a totally new coding style into the mix.

Writing a Standards Document

Okay, so you might agree that standards are a good thing. Now how does a team go about capturing all of their good ideas and optimal design decisions? One approach that my teams and I have used with some success is authoring a rules and guidelines document.

A *rule* is a direction given to developers that must be followed 100% of the time. Usually, for most teams, there are very few hard and fast rules. An enterprise-wide date format could be a valid rule. Using an APEX theme that conforms to the corporate brand standards could be another.

A *guideline* is a direction given to developers that must be followed 80% to 90% of the time. The fact that guidelines are not enforced all of the time is explicit recognition that there are always exception situations. For example, a guideline might direct developers to pass APEX items as parameters when calling a routine in a PL/SQL package. Such a guideline makes sense because it allows the PL/SQL routine to be unit tested without the need of running within the context of an APEX session. An exception to this guideline is often made when the PL/SQL code manipulates an APEX collection.

To be successful, a rules and guidelines document must be crafted in a format that developers will actually use in their daily work. To make this happen, the rules and guidelines document must have the following properties:

- Terse and concise

- Accessible with one or two clicks

- Template driven

- Easily updated and extended

Let's explore these properties.

Terse and Concise

A practical rules and guidelines document is terse and concise, meaning that it is short and says much with few words. The writing style uses short, active voice sentences and bullet points. Screenshots and diagrams are used liberally to illustrate points keeping in mind the trite phrase, "a picture is worth a thousand words". The diagrams can be hand drawn and scanned or photos taken of white board sketches; these are quick and effective so there is no need for fancy, expensive, and time-consuming graphics software. Speed and clarity are highly valued in this environment.

Avoid the 600-page tome syndrome where a heavy document is printed and stored in a fat three ring binder. This strategy is probably worse than writing nothing; writing a fat document is costly to produce and achieves the same result as writing nothing because, in practice, developers will never read a 600-page document that is out of date before the printer ink dries.

Figure 11-3 illustrates the concept. Always search for the "sweet spot" where the documentation is not too little and not too much. At one extreme, you have no standards, which will cause your coding cost to be high due to using a chaotic code base where there is much duplication, inconsistencies, lots of bugs, and reinvented wheels. At the other extreme where you have written and paid for a verbose 600-page standards document, you also will have high coding cost for the very same reasons that you encounter with no standards because the fat document will not be used. A rules and guidelines format will help you find your team's "sweet spot" where you get the biggest bang for your buck.

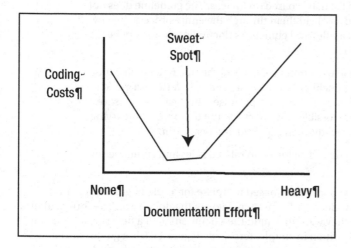

Figure 11-3. *Cost of standards—finding the sweet spot*

Accessible with One or Two Clicks

A rules and guidelines document must be easily accessible so that developers can quickly find searchable guidance. Ideally, the document can be accessed with one or two clicks; for example, it could be in a web document that is kept open in a tab in the developer's browser. This strategy is ideally suited to APEX development since APEX is, of course, a browser-based tool.

Avoid burying your standards in a document management system that requires a login and many navigation clicks. A buried standards document will rarely be dug up.

Template Driven

Use a template. A simple template makes a rule or guideline easy to read and, just as importantly, easy to author. Consistency here is extremely valuable.

A practical template that my teams have used consists of the following headings:

- *Rule/Guideline.* The Rule/Guideline heading is a simple, short, and active-voice statement that describes the main purpose of the rule or guideline.

- *Why.* The Why heading can be one word: "Consistency," for example. Some rules and guidelines will, of course, require more justification. The Why heading is important for developer buy-in. It can also be an important negotiating tool used when other stakeholders challenge the team's strategies. When an external stakeholder wants a feature that you have previously rejected in your selection of an optimum set of strategies, you can win them over to your vision by presenting them with clear, logical, and documented reasoning for why you have chosen your strategy.

- *Result.* The Result heading often contains nothing but a screenshot of the desired result or a snippet of pseudocode. This is frequently all a developer needs to see what result is desired.

- *How.* The How heading documents the details of how a result is to be achieved. Screenshots of the development area with callouts can work well here. You can also use this area as a repository for annotated code snippets that can easily be copied into the working code. For example, experienced APEX developers know exactly how to build a horizontal navigation list that is based on images. The guideline does not need to hold a developer's hand and lead them through the entire process, step by step. It is important to note that a rules and guidelines document should not be an APEX introductory training course.

- *Notes.* The Notes heading is used to document aspects of the rule or guideline that are not obvious. Some rules or guidelines may have side effects. Perhaps a guideline is an imperfect solution based on a technical compromise. This heading can save time by alerting programmers to possible side effects before they waste time trying to solve a tricky problem that has already been explored and dealt with.

- *See Also.* The See Also heading points developers to related rules and guidelines or other documentation sources.

Figure 11-4 illustrates a clean and convenient table-based template for a rule or guideline. This table-based format gives the reader a clean, clear, and consistent view of the document. The format allows authors to simply "fill in the blanks" when they want to extend the document with a new rule or guideline. Figure 11-5 shows you a simple rule that is written in simple, terse text. Figure 11-6 is a guideline that is authored using screenshots. Developers can use the screenshots to achieve their results and the guideline author does not need to spend time writing.

Rule / Guideline	
Why	
Result	
How	
Notes	
See Also	

Figure 11-4. *Rule/guideline table-based template*

Rule	Use formal language of client.
Why	Communicate clearly with no ambiguity.
Result	Formal sentences in the comments.
How	Using English, use formal sentence structure. i.e. begin with a capital letter and end with a period. No slang. Use active voice sentence structure: Subject (the doer) – Verb (the action) – Predicate (the thing acted upon) – Condition (optional) Examples of active voice: The child threw the ball. The read-only user can update this field when the moon is full. This process deletes this record when the status is DELETE or DEPRECATED. Examples of passive voice: The ball was thrown by the child. This field can by updated when the moon is full by the read-only user. When the status is either DELETE or DEPRECATED then this record is deleted by this process.
Notes	
See Also	

Figure 11-5. *An example of a rule*

Guideline	Use the Attribute Dictionary for columns that are common to many tables.
Why	Consistency.
Result	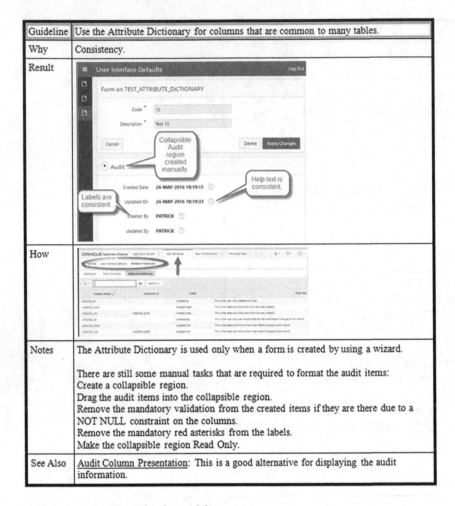
How	
Notes	The Attribute Dictionary is used only when a form is created by using a wizard. There are still some manual tasks that are required to format the audit items: Create a collapsible region. Drag the audit items into the collapsible region. Remove the mandatory validation from the created items if they are there due to a NOT NULL constraint on the columns. Remove the mandatory red asterisks from the labels. Make the collapsible region Read Only.
See Also	Audit Column Presentation: This is a good alternative for displaying the audit information.

Figure 11-6. *An example of a guideline*

Easily Updated and Extended

Development teams, technology, and application requirements do not stand still. They all continually evolve and, especially in the computer world, they evolve very rapidly. Sometimes the changes are predicted ahead of time, but often everyone is surprised and shocked by dramatic changes that unceremoniously kick people out of their comfort zones. The bottom line here is the fact that today's development standards can become outdated in a very short period of time. Using outdated standards will make you and your team uncompetitive, which is not a very good place to be.

In this type of environment, your standards will be subjected to continuous reviews, updates, deletions, and additions. To support this activity, you need a documentation technology that enables your team to update its standards almost in real time without a lot of bureaucratic overhead. An ideal tool for this task is Google Docs.

Google Docs

Google Docs is a practical tool for authoring standards that are subject to frequent updates. The Google Docs properties that make it well suited for template-based standards in a dynamic software development environment are:

- Cloud file storage

- Web-based

- Editing, suggesting, and viewing modes

- Multiple simultaneous editors

Cloud file storage makes your standards documents available to your entire team no matter where they are located in the world.

Google Docs is a *web-based* technology. This feature is especially attractive to APEX development teams whose main development tool is a web browser. Developers can easily configure a browser tab that contains their rules and guidelines document for quick reference.

Google Docs provides *editing, suggesting, and viewing modes.* Figure 11-7 illustrates how a person selects an editing mode. The original author of a document shares the document with individual team members. The author gives team members document update privileges that are appropriate to their role. The editing mode gives a team member full control over the document. Editing mode is given to a small number of senior team members who are have been selected to be on a standards committee. Ideally this committee should meet weekly to evaluate suggestions from the rest of the team and keep the standards document up to date. Suggestion mode is used to add, update, or delete content plus add comments. Figure 11-8 shows suggestion mode in action, where a developer has added a good suggestion as a paragraph and the standards committee has responded with a series of comments that lead to an action item. Viewing mode allows a reader to see the most recent "approved" version of the document without the clutter of the most recent suggestions and comments. The "approved" version is the original draft plus all of the cumulative suggestions that have been accepted by the standards committee.

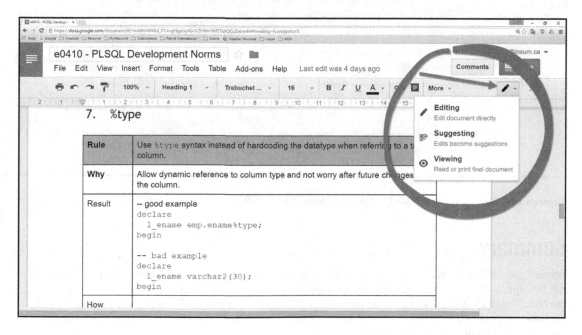

Figure 11-7. *Google Docs update modes*

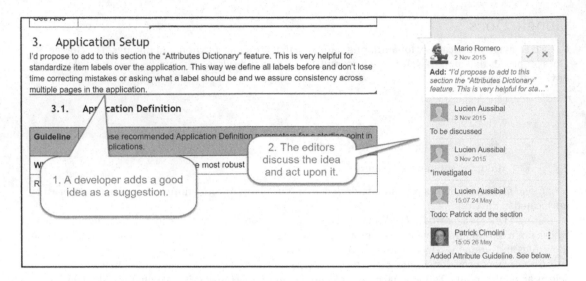

Figure 11-8. *Google Docs suggestion mode in action*

Multiple simultaneous editors can update a Google document in real time. There is no need for tedious check-out and check-in procedures. Figure 11-9 shows what happens when two or more persons are editing or making suggestions in a Google Docs document simultaneously. An icon is displayed in the header area with the person's Google photo or avatar. You can also see what the second person is typing and exactly where the second person's cursor is located. This feature is valuable because it lets a person know who else is editing the document at the same time and it can be used when remote standards committee members are reviewing a document at the same time using remote screen-sharing technology.

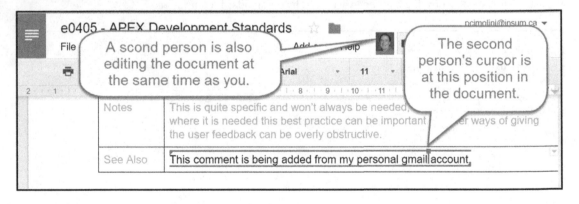

Figure 11-9. *Two people editing a Google Docs document simultaneously*

Summary

Written standards are required to keep a team pulling together efficiently and effectively. Writing standards can be expensive and time consuming, so care must be taken to devote the appropriate amount of effort to the task. The rules and guidelines framework, when authored using Google Docs as a word processor and document repository, provides a practical and cost-effective methodology for capturing, publishing, and updating a team's optimal set of standards.

APPENDIX A

■ ■ ■

A Cloudy Crystal Ball

How long will Oracle Application Express (APEX) be around? It is now pushing 15 years old, which makes it "long in the tooth". Here is my two cents on the future of APEX.

Often, software tools become unusable when their underlying system platform changes. For example, Oracle Forms has had a long and successful life, as a development tool that was built on top of a client/server architectural platform. It did not make a clean transition into the web environment because the client/server architecture was baked into its fundamental design. Therefore, in our current web-based world, it is being replaced by tools, like APEX, that are web-based.

APEX, too, will be replaced if and when the web, as we know it today, is replaced by a radically different technology. I suspect that a replacement for the web is in the far distant future because an incredible amount of web hardware and software infrastructure is currently in place all over the world. This will not be easy to swap out.

Having said that, I believe APEX has a bright and possible long-lived future.

In the present, APEX has become a popular tool that is used by many businesses, both large and small. On the large end of the scale, major banks and government departments have built many APEX applications that have become mission critical. At the small end of the scale, I have worked with small departments and companies that have built APEX applications inside their firewalls using the combination of APEX and OracleXE, the free Oracle database. Today, APEX has become the tool of choice to many organizations that use Oracle databases. Oracle itself had invested heavily in APEX applications; The Oracle Store at `https://shop.oracle.com/apex/f?p=dstore:home:0` is an example of Oracle reliance on APEX to deliver important public facing information. A blog post by Joel Kallman, Director of Software Development at Oracle, documents Oracle's heavy reliance on APEX; over 2,000 distinct APEX application support over 18,000 Oracle employees. The blog post is found at `http://joelkallman.blogspot.ca/2014/05/oracle-application-express-fast-like.html`.

In the near future, say the five-year horizon, I see no change. APEX has enough momentum to carry it though the next five years as a "force to be reckoned with".

In ten years? Then the crystal ball starts to become a wee bit cloudy. What advances will pop out of the labs of the big players like Oracle? What will pop out of an obscure garage and storm the world like Google did? However, given the weight of the current web infrastructure, I suspect that there is a good probability that APEX, in its future form, will still be around and thriving in ten years' time.

What will APEX look like in ten years? I cannot guess. Instead, I will defer to Mike Hichwa, the father of APEX, who voiced his vision for APEX at the APEX Connect 2016 conference in Berlin, Germany in his presentation, "APEX Vision, past, Present, Future". A `youtube.com` video of this event is available at:

`https://www.youtube.com/watch?v=i_5OUipxSEY`

This presentation is definitely worth your time if you are interested in the future of APEX.

© Patrick Cimolini 2017

P. Cimolini, *Oracle Application Express by Design*, https://doi.org/10.1007/978-1-4842-2427-4_12

APPENDIX B

■ ■ ■

Things Not Covered

This book's intent was to fill an APEX niche that has not, to my knowledge, been filled. There are areas that are not covered in this book. You might think that, to be complete, this book should address them; however, many of these areas are already well documented in the literature and I am loath to duplicate the existing work. The APEX home page on the Oracle Technology Network (OTN) site contains an up-to-date list of APEX books plus links to many helpful blogs. The following areas are well documented on the Community page on the APEX site.

- Security. Security cannot be ignored. In my opinion, there are two books that are "must reads" for serious APEX developers. They are *Expert Oracle Application Security* by Scott Spendolini (Apress) and *Hands-On Oracle Application Express Security* by Recx. There are two security products in the marketplace that analyze an APEX application's export file for security issues. They are APEX-SERT (http://www.oraopensource.com/apex-sert/) and ApexSec (https://apexsec.recx.co.uk/). You must use one of these tools as part of your Quality Assurance process.

- APEX Installation.

- Application promotion from DEV to TEST to STAGE to PROD.

- Coding best practices.

- PDF printing. There are a number of PDF printing technologies that work well with APEX:

    - Oracle BI Publisher: http://www.oracle.com/technetwork/middleware/bi-publisher/overview/index.html

    - APEX Office Print (AOP): https://www.apexofficeprint.com/index.html

    - PL/PDF: http://plpdf.com/

    - JasperReports: https://community.jaspersoft.com/

    - Oracle REST Data Services (ORDS): http://www.oracle.com/technetwork/developer-tools/rest-data-services/overview/index.html

    - Apache FOP: https://xmlgraphics.apache.org/fop/

- Project and team management.

- Testing web applications.

- Multi-lingual applications.

- Source code control.

© Patrick Cimolini 2017
P. Cimolini, *Oracle Application Express by Design*, https://doi.org/10.1007/978-1-4842-2427-4_13

- Legal issues. This topic is not documented on the APEX site. An example of a legal issue is a server's physical location, which can be a very sensitive issue for the off-shore banking industry, especially in a cloud environment. A chat with your company's legal department may surface legal issues that may not be obvious to the technical teams.

Index

Get the eBook for only $5!

Why limit yourself?

With most of our titles available in both PDF and ePUB format, you can access your content wherever and however you wish—on your PC, phone, tablet, or reader.

Since you've purchased this print book, we are happy to offer you the eBook for just $5.

To learn more, go to http://www.apress.com/companion or contact support@apress.com.

Apress®

〈IOUG〉 independent oracle users group — *For the Complete Technology & Database Professional*

IOUG represents the **voice of Oracle technology and database professionals** - empowering you to be **more productive** in your business and career by **delivering education,** sharing **best practices** and providing technology direction and **networking opportunities.**

Context, Not Just Content

IOUG is dedicated to helping our members become an #IOUGenius by staying on the cutting-edge of Oracle technologies and industry issues through practical content, user-focused education, and invaluable networking and leadership opportunities:

- *SELECT Journal* is our quarterly publication that provides in-depth, peer-reviewed articles on industry news and best practices in Oracle technology

- Our #IOUGenius blog highlights a featured weekly topic and provides content driven by Oracle professionals and the IOUG community

- Special Interest Groups provide you the chance to collaborate with peers on the specific issues that matter to you and even take on leadership roles outside of your organization

- COLLABORATE is our once-a-year opportunity to connect with the members of not one, but three, Oracle users groups (IOUG, OAUG and Quest) as well as with the top names and faces in the Oracle community.

Who we are...

... more than 20,000 database professionals, developers, application and infrastructure architects, business intelligence specialists and IT managers

... a community of users that share experiences and knowledge on issues and technologies that matter to you and your organization

Interested? Join IOUG's community of Oracle technology and database professionals at **www.ioug.org/Join.**

Independent Oracle Users Group | phone: (312) 245-1579 | email: membership@ioug.org
330 N. Wabash Ave., Suite 2000, Chicago, IL 60611

Printed in the United States
By Bookmasters